Progressive
Scales and Modes
For Guitar

By
Peter Gelling

Visit our Website
www.koalamusicpublications.com

The Progressive Series of Music Instruction Books, CDs, Videos and DVDs

Published by
KOALA MUSIC PUBLICATIONS

PROGRESSIVE SCALES & MODES FOR GUITAR
I.S.B.N. 978 1 86469 058 9
Order Code: CP-69058
Acknowledgments
Cover Photograph: Phil Martin
Photographs: Phil Martin

For more information on this series contact;
Koala Music Publications
email: info@koalamusicpublications.com
or visit our website;
www.koalamusicpublications.com

Contents

Introduction

Progressive Scales and Modes for Guitar is more than just a reference book of scales and modes. This book gives you a complete system for learning any scale, mode or chord, based on the five most common chord shapes. This enables you to easily memorise any new sound and to build a solid visual and aural foundation for everything you play. The book also shows you **how to use each scale** as well as how and why it fits with a particular chord or progression. The final section contains "jam along" progressions for every scale presented in the book so you can try out all the licks you have learnt, and also practice improvising with each of the scales.

The book is divided into four main sections. **SECTION 1** deals with the major scale in the open position and shows how seven different modes can be derived from it. It also gives the formulas for constructing modes and chords as well as demonstrating how and why each mode works against a particular chord or progression. Techniques for practicing scales and creating melodies are shown to help you make music from each mode instead of just running up and down the scales. Section 1 ends with a solo using alll seven modes derived from the major scale.

SECTION 2 demontrates moveable fingerings for all seven of the modes learnt in section 1. Each fingering is closely related to one of five basic open chord shapes, making memorisation easy. Several typical licks are given along with each mode to help you identify the character of each mode as well as give you ideas for improvising. Sequence patterns for practicing each fingering are given, along with demonstrations of how to play them in any key.

SECTION 3 Shows all the fingering patterns for the minor key scales. Once again, typical licks are given with each scale to show you how the scales can be used to make music.

SECTION 4 deals with pentatonic scales and the Blues scales, along with the whole tone scale and the diminished scale. This section also contains jam along progressions for all of the scales and modes introduced in the earlier sections. Once you know all of the scales presented in the book, and how to use them, you should be confident improvising over any chord or progression as well as knowing which sounds work best in any style of music.

Using the Compact Disc

It is recommended that you have a copy of the accompanying compact disc that includes all the examples in this book. The book shows you where to put your fingers and what technique to use and the recording lets you hear how each example should sound. Practice the examples slowly at first, gradually increasing tempo. Once you are confident you can play the example evenly without stopping the beat, try playing along with the recording. You will hear a drum beat at the beginning of each example, to lead you into the example and to help you keep time. A small diagram of a compact disc with a number as shown below indicates a recorded example. Some of the tracks on the CD contain more than one example. In these cases, index points are used (1.0, 1.1, 1.3 etc). If your CD player has an index points function, you can select each example individually. If not, each example will automatically follow the previous one. The first track on the CD contains the tuning notes for the six open strings of the Guitar. 1.0 is the open 6th string (Low E note), 1.1 is the open 5th string (A note) etc.

1.0 ⟵——— CD Track Number

Fretboard Diagrams

Fretboard diagrams are given throughout this book to show which patterns and fingerings are given for each scale or mode. To know how to read the diagrams, study the following illustration.

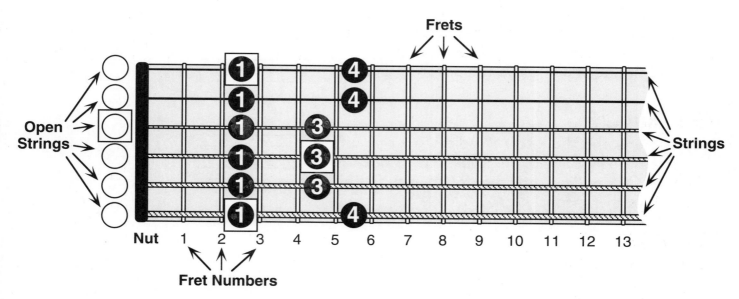

● or ○ = A note used in the scale or pattern.

[●] or [○] = Indicates the note is the key note of the scale.

[②] = The number refers to the left hand fingering.

Left Hand Fingering

❶ Index Finger
❷ Middle Finger
❸ Ring Finger
❹ Little Finger

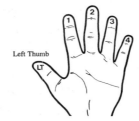

Tablature

This book uses standard music notation and tablature notation. If you cannot read music notes, use the tab written below the music. Music readers will need to look at the tab to see what technique is being used to play certain notes (e.g. hammer-on, slide etc).

Tablature is a method of indicating the position of notes on the fretboard. There are six "tab" lines each representing one of the six strings on the guitar.

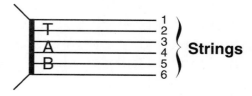

When a number is placed on one of the lines, it indicates the fret location of the note e.g.

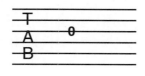

This indicates the **seventh** fret of the **5th** string (an **E** note).

This indicates the **3rd** string open (a **G** note).

Tablature Symbols

The following tablature symbols will appear throughout this book.

The Hammer-On

A curved line and the letter H indicates a hammer-on. The first note is played but the second note is produced by hammering on the left hand finger, which plays the second note.

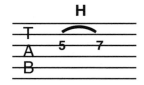 

The Pull-Off

A curved line and the letter P indicates a pull-off. The first note is played but the second note is produced by pulling off the left hand finger, which plays the second note.

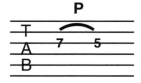 

The Slide

The letter S and a straight line indicates a slide. If the line comes from below the number, slide from a lower fret but if the line is above the number, slide from a higher fret. The bracketed number in the tab is the fret to slide from.

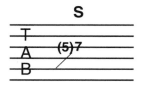 

The Bend

The letter B and a curved line represents a bend. The note is played by the left hand finger which bends the string (from the note indicated in the tab to the pitch of the note in brackets).

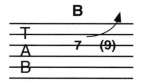 

The Release Bend

A curved line on the top left hand side of the number and the letter R indicates a release bend. This technique involves bending the note indicated with the left hand (from the pitch of the note in brackets), playing the string whilst bent, then returning the string to its normal position. The release bend creates a drop in pitch from a higher note to a lower note.

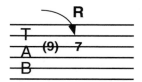 

Vibrato

A wavy line shown above the note indicates when vibrato is used. Vibrato is controlled with the left hand finger which is fretting the note. As the finger frets the note, move the finger rapidly back and forth in the direction of the adjacent strings.

The Trail Off

After playing a specific note, slide away from the note, gradually releasing the pressure off the fretting hand. A trail off is indicated by a wavy line moving diagonally away from the right hand side of the note.

SECTION 1
Modes and the Major Scale

The Major Scale

The C Major Scale

A major scale is a pattern of eight notes in alphabetical order that produce the familiar sound:

Do Re Mi Fa So La Ti Do

The C major scale contains these notes in the following order:

C   D   <u>E   F</u>   G   A   <u>B   C</u>

The distance between each note is two frets except for <u>**EF**</u> and <u>**BC**</u> where the distance is only one fret.

The distance of two frets is called a **tone** indicated by **T**.

The distance of one fret is called a **semitone** indicated by **ST**.

The major scale is probably the most common scale used in music. Written below is one octave of the C major scale in the open position.

 2

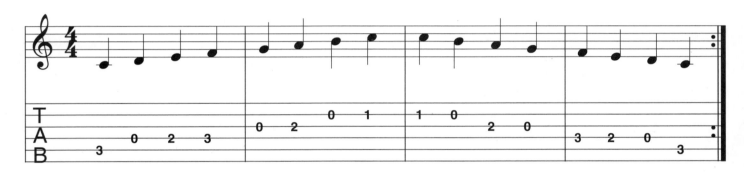

Below is a diagram of all of the natural notes in the open position. They are all notes of the C major scale, even though the lowest note of the pattern is E and the highest note is G. The key note **C** is indicated twice. This pattern can be described as the full open position fingering of the C major scale.

C Major Scale in Open Position

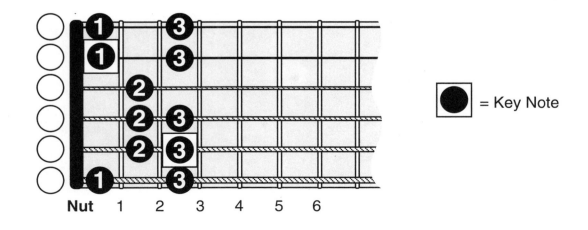

Here are the notes from the diagram written in standard music notation and tablature.

3

These notes can be used to play literally thousands of melodies in the key of C major. It is not necessary to always start and finish on the note C. Depending on which chords you are playing over, it may sound best to start on **any** of the notes in the scale. E.g. if you were playing over a C chord followed by a D minor chord you could play the scale starting on C for the C chord but start on D for the D minor chord, as shown in the following example. This is a **modal** approach to playing scales.

4

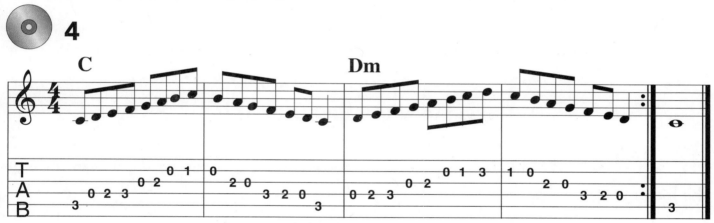

Preparation for Modes

Using modes to play over chord progressions means finding the best group of notes to play over each particular chord. There are seven different notes in a major scale and each of these notes can be used as the starting note for a different mode. Here is an exercise to help you become familiar with the positions of all of the notes within the open position fingering of the C major scale.

5

Modes

As mentioned on the previous page there are seven different modes which can be derived from the major scale by starting on each of the seven notes of the major scale. These modes were first used in ancient Greece and have been widely used throughout history in all types of music. They are particularly useful for improvising or composing melodies over chord progressions. The names of the seven modes and their relationship to the major scale are shown below.

1. Ionian mode – The Ionian mode is another name for the major scale itself. By starting and ending on the first note of the major scale (C) you can play the Ionian mode.

C Ionian = C D E F G A B C

2. Dorian mode – The Dorian mode starts and ends on the second note of the major scale (in this case D).

D Dorian = D E F G A B C D

3. Phrygian mode – The Phrygian mode starts and ends on the third note of the major scale (in this case E).

E Phrygian = E F G A B C D E

4. Lydian mode – The Lydian mode starts and ends on the fourth note of the major scale (in this case F).

F Lydian = F G A B C D E F

5. Mixolydian mode – The Mixolydian mode starts and ends on the fifth note of the major scale (in this case G).

G Mixolydian = G A B C D E F G

6. Aeolian mode – The Aeolian mode starts and ends on the sixth note of the major scale (in this case A).

A Aeolian = A B C D E F G A

7. Locrian mode – The Locrian mode starts and ends on the seventh note of the major scale (in this case B).

B Locrian = B C D E F G A B

6

Here is an exercise containing all of the modes derived from the major scale. Listen to the sound of each mode against the chords indicated above the music.

Once you know the notes contained within each mode, it is a good idea to practice them over two octaves wherever possible. This becomes easier when modes are applied to moveable fingerings (see section 2) but it is also possible for some of the modes in the open position. The following example shows the E Phrygian mode shown in two octaves. Notice that this involves all the natural notes in the open position.

7

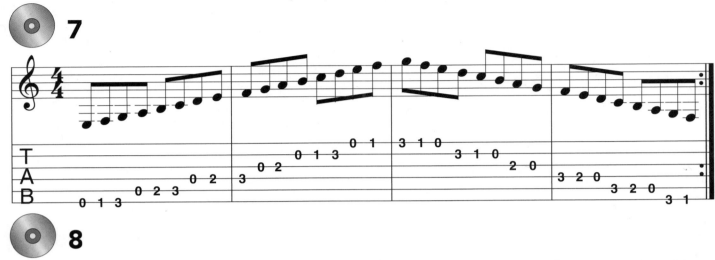

8

Once you are comfortable with each octave of a mode, try putting them together. Here is the F Lydian mode in two octaves played separately and then consecutively.

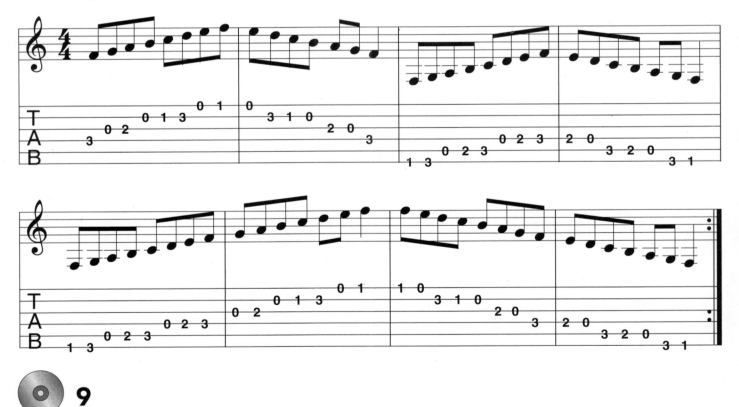

9

This next example shows the G Mixolydian mode played over two octaves.

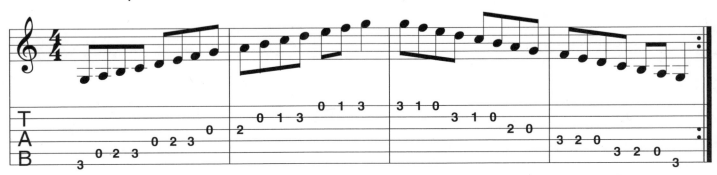

Scale Tone Chords

As well as modes being created from the seven notes of the major scale, it is also possible to create a chord from each note of the scale. By taking the **first**, **third** and **fifth** notes of each mode, there are **triads** (3 note chords) which can be derived from the major scale. Listed below are the seven modes and the triad created from each mode.

C Ionian = C D E F G A B C   **C Major Triad = C   E   G**

D Dorian = D E F G A B C D   **D Minor Triad = D   F   A**

E Phrygian = E F G A B C D E   **E Minor Triad = E   G   B**

F Lydian = F G A B C D E F   **F Major Triad = F   A   C**

G Mixolydian = G A B C D E F G   **G Major Triad = G   B   D**

A Aeolian = A B C D E F G A   **A Minor Triad = A   C   E**

B Locrian = B C D E F G A B   **B Diminished Triad = B   D   F**

Because each mode contains three notes from its corresponding triad, the modes work particularly well when played against these chords. Using modes to play over chords means it is possible to create melodies which are very specific to certain chords. It is possible to use the C major scale freely over any chord in the key of C major, but the C Ionian mode is very specific to the C major triad. If you had a chord progression containing the chords C, F and G you could simply play the C major scale (C Ionian) or you could use the F Lydian mode over the F chord and the G Mixolydian mode over the G chord. Here are some examples.

 10

Here is a melody using the C Ionian mode over the chords C, F and G in the key of C.

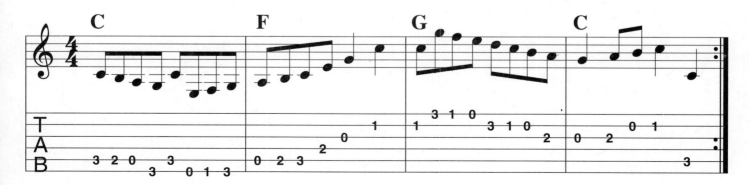

The melody used in example 10 sounds reasonably good but it doesn't fit the chord progression perfectly. Here is the same progression with the Ionian, Lydian and Mixolydian modes played over it. Listen to how well each mode fits its particular chord.

11

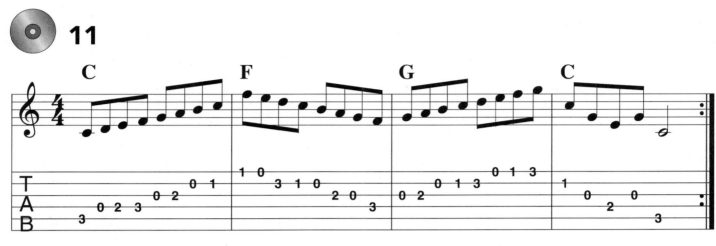

12

Now try this melody created from the modes in the previous example. Listen to how much better this melody fits the chords than the one in example 10.

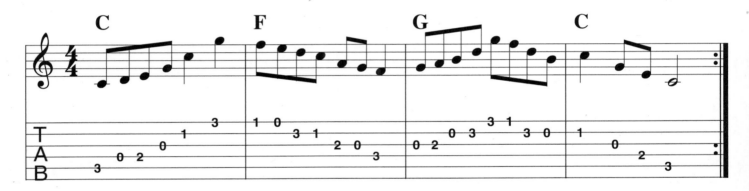

Even though all of the modes in this section are derived from the C major scale, it is possible to create sound from some of the modes which are very different to the major scale. Listen to the Spanish type of sound produced by the E Phrygian mode in the following example.

13

 **14**

This next example demonstrates the type of sound produced by the Aeolian mode. This mode is also known as the **Natural Minor** scale and can be used over chord progressions in minor keys. All of these modes can be used as a tonality in themselves rather than always being played against chords in a related major key. This subject will be dealt with in more detail in section 2.

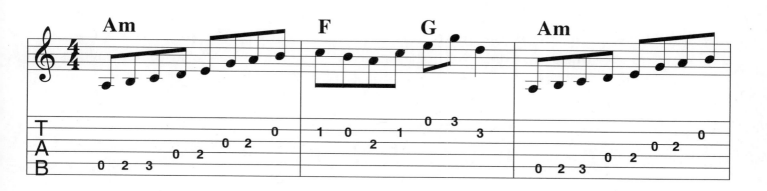

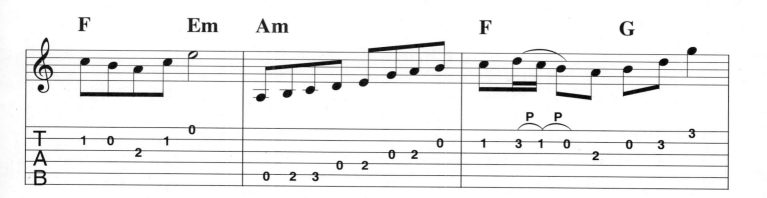

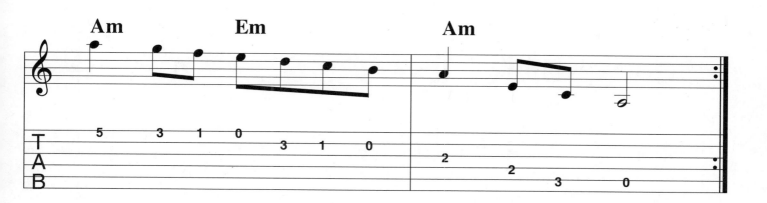

More on Modes and Chords

In Jazz, Blues, Funk, Rock, Latin and many other styles there are chords used which contain more than three notes. By taking a triad and adding other notes on top of it, a variety of other chords can be created. The most common of these are seventh chords. A seventh chord can be created by adding the seventh note of a mode to the basic triad. The type of seventh chord this creates will depend on the notes contained in both the mode it is derived from and the basic triad. This can be confusing at first, so it is worth looking at the theory of chords and modes to identify the basic principles of chord and mode construction.

The Chromatic Scale

The chromatic scale contains every possible note used in western music. All of its notes are one semitone apart (on the guitar a semitone is one fret). The degrees of the major scale can be identified by using the numbers 1 to 7 as shown below in the C major scale (C Ionian) which contains all of the natural notes (natural meaning no sharps or flats).

C Major Scale

C	D	E	F	G	A	B	C
1	2	3	4	5	6	7	8

By adding all of the possible extra notes in between the natural notes of the C major scale, the **C chromatic scale** is created.

C Chromatic Scale

C C#/Db D D#/Eb E F F#/Gb G G#/Ab A A#/Bb B C

The "in between" notes can be described as either sharps or flats. Because of the way modes and chords are constructed, flats are used more often than sharps. Here once again is the C chromatic scale with scale degrees written under the notes. The scale degrees written here relate to the natural notes and the flat notes. The sharps are enharmonic equivalents, which means they are the same pitch (e.g C# =Db and F# =Gb).

C C#/Db D D#/Eb E F F#/Gb G G#/Ab A A#/Bb B C

| 1 | b2 | 2 | b3 | 3 | 4 | b5 | 5 | b6 | 6 | b7 | 7 | 1 |

As mentioned earlier, is is possible to create many different types of chords by adding notes on top of triads. E.g. by adding the 7th degree of the scale to a C major triad, the C major seventh chord is created (Cmaj7). However, by adding the flattened 7th degree to the same C major triad, the C seventh chord is created (C7). By flattening the 3rd degree of the C major triad, it becomes a C minor triad (Cm). By adding a flattened 7th degree to the C minor triad, a C minor seventh chord (Cm7) is created. Many chords can be created by slight variations to these basic chords. The combination of degrees used in any chord is called the **chord formula**. The formulas for the most common types of chords are shown on the following page along with an example of each chord as they relate to the key of C.

Major Chord Formula

Chord Symbol

C

1   3   5

Notes in Chord

C	E	G
1	3	5

Minor Chord Formula

Chord Symbol

Cm

1   ♭3   5

Notes in Chord

C	E♭	G
1	♭3	5

Diminished Chord Formula

Chord Symbol

C°

1   ♭3   ♭5

Notes in Chord

C	E♭	G♭
1	♭3	♭5

Augmented Chord Formula

Chord Symbol

C+

1   3   ♯5

Notes in Chord

C	E	G♯
1	3	♯5

Major Seventh Chord Formula

Chord Symbol

CMaj7

1   3   5   7

Notes in Chord

C	E	G	B
1	3	5	7

Seventh Chord Formula

Chord Symbol

C7

1   3   5   ♭7

Notes in Chord

C	E	G	B♭
1	3	5	♭7

Minor Seventh Chord Formula

Chord Symbol

Cm7

1   ♭3   5   ♭7

Notes in Chord

C	E♭	G	B♭
1	♭3	5	♭7

Minor Seven Flat Five Chord Formula

Chord Symbol

Cm7♭5

1   ♭3   ♭5   ♭7

Notes in Chord

C	E♭	G♭	B♭
1	♭3	♭5	♭7

These are just the most common chords used in music, there are many other extensions and variations as well. (for more information on chords and chord formulas, see *Progressive Jazz Guitar*).

18

By applying the formulas for seventh chords to the C major scale, the following series of chords is created. These are called **scale tone seventh chords**.

Cmaj7 Dm7 Em7 Fmaj7 G7 Am7 Bm7♭5

$\overline{1}$ $\overline{11}$ $\overline{111}$ $\overline{IV}$ $\overline{V}$ $\overline{VI}$ $\overline{V11}$

When numbering chords within a key, Roman numerals are used. This makes it clear that a chord is being described rather than a single note (scale degree) which would be indicated by a number (1, 2, ♭3, ♯4 etc).

 15

Example 15 shows the seven modes derived from the C major scale played against the seven scale tone seventh chords from the key of C major.

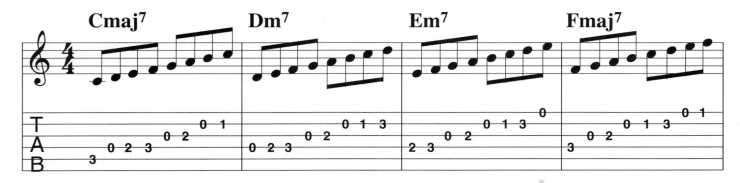

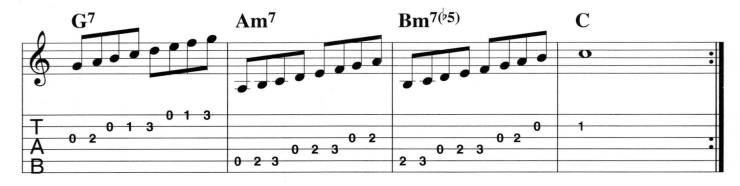

 16

Because each seventh chord contains four notes of the mode it relates to, modes work extremely well over seventh chords. Listen to the sound of this line using the D Dorian mode over a Dm7 chord. Try playing some of the other examples you have learnt against seventh chords as well as experimenting and creating some of your own melodies.

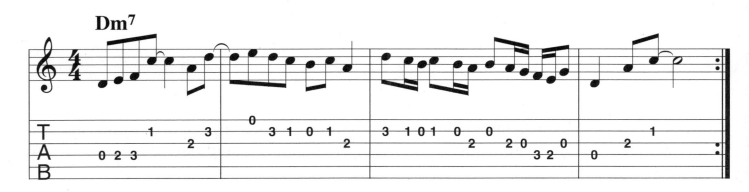

Sequences

One of the best ways to practice scales and modes is the use of sequences. A **sequence** is a repetitive pattern in which the rhythm remains the same while the pitches are repeated higher or lower, usually within a specific scale or mode. Practicing sequences will help you to become more familiar with the scale or mode you are learning as well as enabling you to create melodies more easily instead of just running up and down the scale. Here are some sequences within the C major scale.

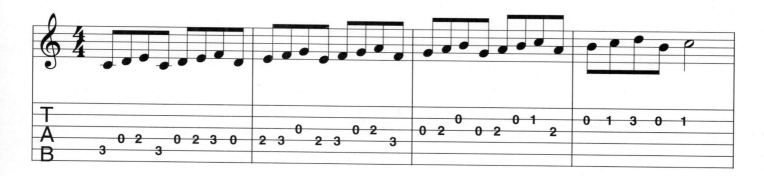

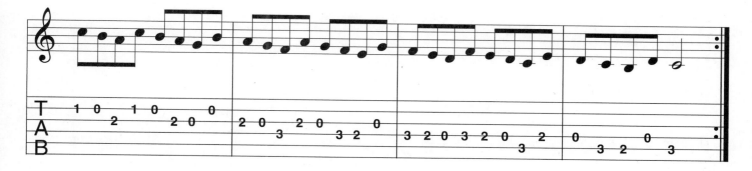

This sequence uses intervals of a 3rd. Using all of the intervals up to an octave is an excellent way of becoming familiar with the musical possibilities of a scale. (For more on intervals see *Progressive Jazz Lead Guitar Method*.)

19

This sequence covers all of the notes in the modes you have learnt. It is a good idea to practice any sequence across an entire fingering pattern.

Another important thing to keep in mind when practicing scales and modes is to use a variety of rhythms. Here is a sequence which applies a triplet pattern to the A Aeolian mode.

20

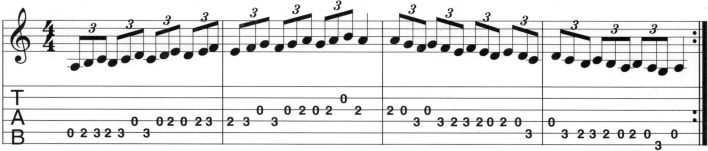

21

This sequence also uses notes in groups of three, but contains an eighth note and two sixteenth notes instead of the triplet.

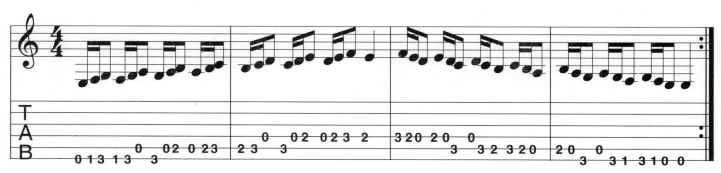

22

One of the most common ways sequences are used in music is as a **riff**. A riff is a sequence which fits a specific chord or progression. A riff can be a set rhythm (exact repetition) or it can be altered to fit various chords. Here is a one bar riff applied to a chord progression which is derived from the A Aeolian mode. (For more on riffs and set rhythms, see *Progressive Blues Lead Guitar Technique*).

23

To end this section, here is a solo which uses all of the natural notes contained in the various modes you have learnt and is played over a chord progression which fits all seven of the modes. The backing for this solo is also used as a jam along progression on the accompanying recording (see page 83). Use it to practice improvising with the major scale and its modes.

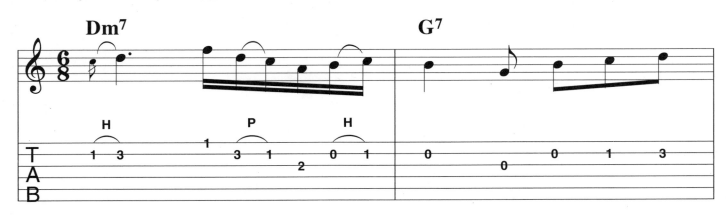

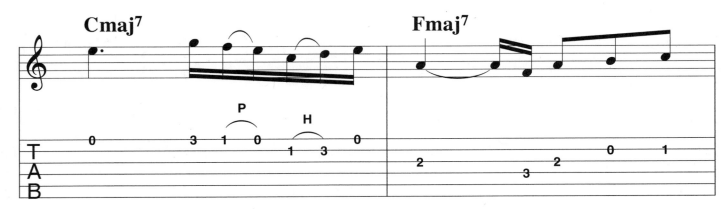

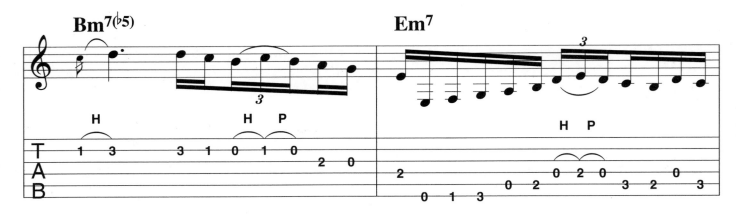

SECTION 2
Modes Along the Fretboard

Mode Formulas

In section 1 you learnt all of the modes derived from the major scale. Each of these modes can be played in many different positions on the fretboard and can be played in any key. Just as there are twelve major keys, there are also twelve possible starting notes for each of the modes. Any note of the chromatic scale can be used as a starting note for any mode. This requires a knowedge of the formula for each mode. The scale degrees of each mode are listed below.

Ionian = 1 2 3 4 5 6 7

Dorian = 1 2 ♭3 4 5 6 ♭7

Phrygian = 1 ♭2 ♭3 4 5 ♭6 ♭7

Lydian = 1 2 3 ♯4 5 6 7

Mixolydian = 1 2 3 4 5 6 ♭7

Aeolian = 1 2 ♭3 4 5 ♭6 ♭7 — *pure minor or natural minor scale*

Locrian = 1 ♭2 ♭3 4 ♭5 ♭6 ♭7

harmonic minor (malmsteen)
aeolian Δ c raised 7
melodic minor (fusion/jazz)
aeolian Δ c raised 6 + 7

If you are serious about using modes in your playing it will be necessary to memorise the formula for each of these modes. Don't try to memorise them all at once, take one mode at a time and learn the formula as it relates to the **sound** of the mode. Learn the fingerings for the mode and experiment with it. Learn the licks which are given at the end of each group of fingerings and then listen to your favourite recordings and try learning some solos which use each mode. In this book all of the scales and modes are written with C as the starting note, as this makes it easy to compare the modes. However, it is important to eventually learn all modes in all keys. All you need to work out a mode in any key is the starting note and the formula. Here is the Dorian mode shown in four different keys.

C Dorian = C D E♭ F G A B♭
           1 2 ♭3 4 5 6 ♭7

F Dorian = F G A♭ B♭ C D E♭
           1 2 ♭3 4 5 6 ♭7

A Dorian = A B C D E F♯ G
           1 2 ♭3 4 5 6 ♭7

B Dorian = B C♯ D E F♯ G♯ A
           1 2 ♭3 4 5 6 ♭7

Moveable Fingerings

For each mode there are five basic moveable fingering patterns which can be moved to any part of the fretboard. These fingerings can be named according to the chord shape to which each fingering corresponds. The names of the five forms (formations or patterns) are easy to memorise because they spell the word **CAGED** when put together. It is the position of the keynotes in each fingering which determines the name of the form. End to end these five forms cover the whole fretboard before repeating. The fingerings of these forms are shown below for the C Ionian mode along with the chord shapes to which they relate. (For a more detailed demonstration of the five scale forms, see *Progressive Blues Lead Guitar Method*).

Open Chord Shape

Chord Form

Ionian Scale Form

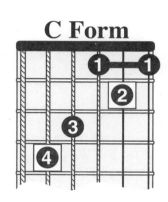

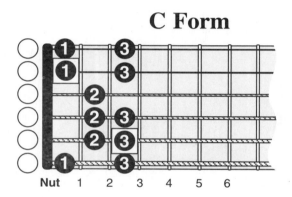

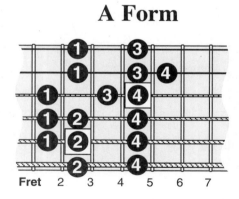

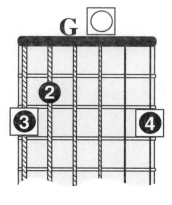

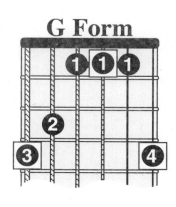

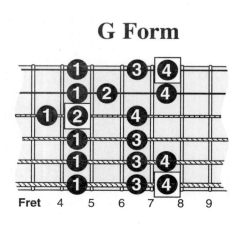

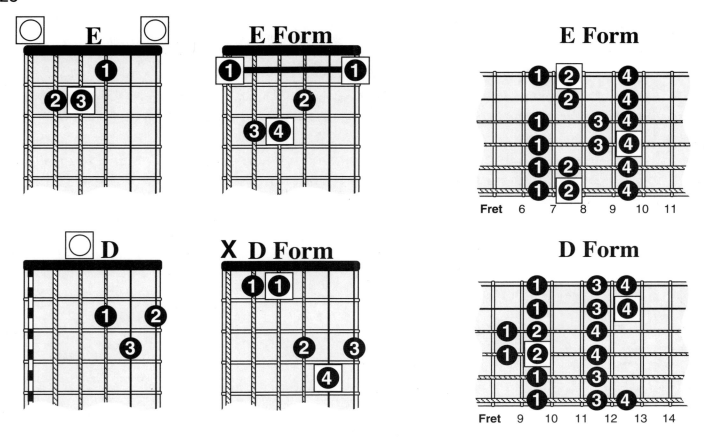

The following diagram shows how the five forms cover the whole fretboard when placed end to end.

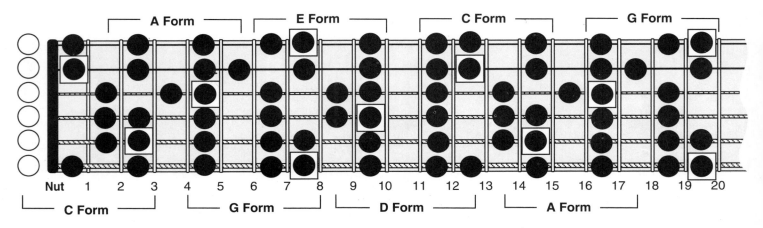

Let's look at each of the five scale forms individually. The diagram below shows the **C form** of the Ionian mode. This is the open position major scale you learnt in section 1.

C Form

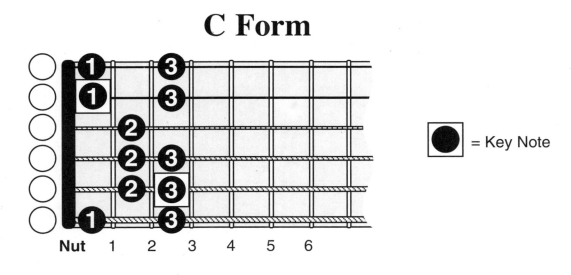

● = Key Note

A Form

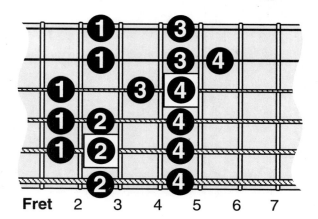

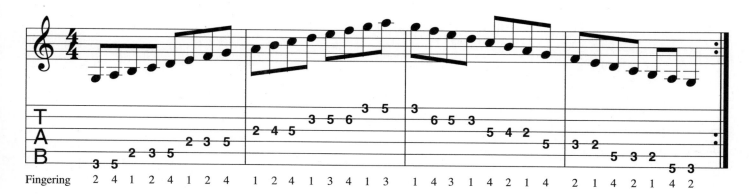

G Form

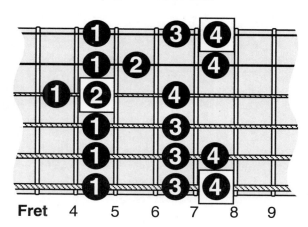

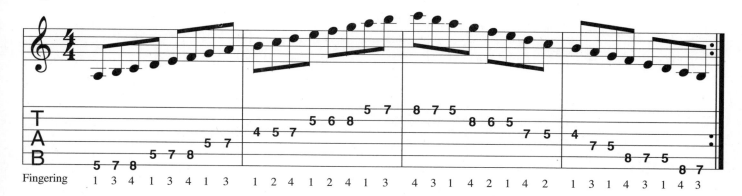

E Form

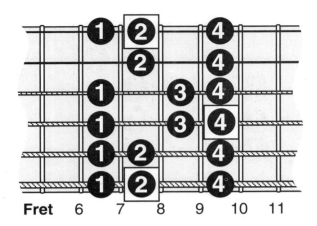

24.2

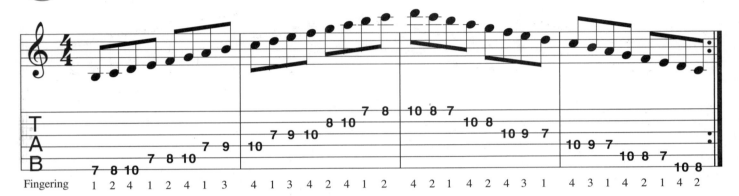

D Form

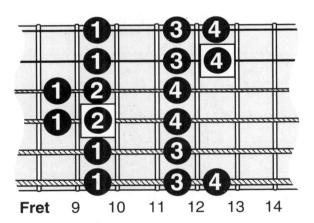

24.3

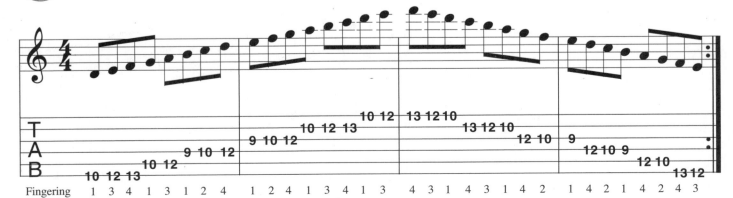

Progressing still higher up the fretboard, here is the C form an octave higher than the open position C form. At this point the pattern of five forms begins to repeat.

C Form

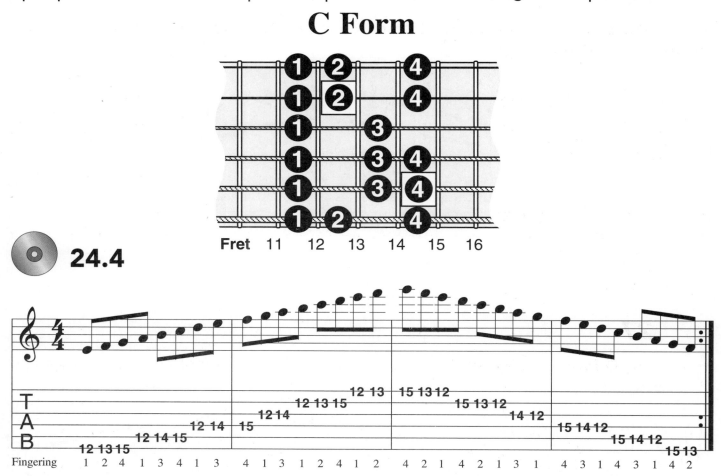

24.4

You have now learnt all five forms of the C Ionian mode. Because each of these fingerings is moveable, it is possible to play them in any key. All you need to do is to locate the root note (or keynote) and then follow the correct fingering. E.g. once you know that the root notes for a C form scale are always on the 5th and 2nd strings, you just find the note of the key you wish to play in on either of those strings. Example 25 shows the moveable C form fingering of the **D Ionian** mode, which is in the second position.

25

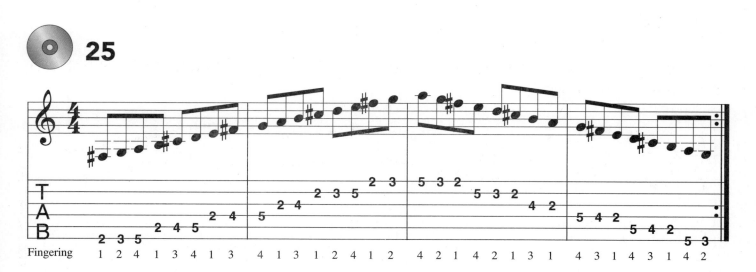

26

Here is the **E form** of **A Ionian**. The E form can always be identified by the root notes on the 6th, 4th and 1st strings.

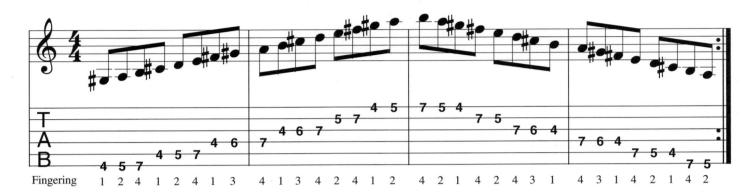

Fingering   1 2 4 1 2 4 1 3   4 1 3 4 2 4 1 2   4 2 1 4 2 4 3 1   4 3 1 4 2 1 4 2

27

Here is the **D form** of **G Ionian**. The D form is identified by the root notes on the 4th and 2nd strings.

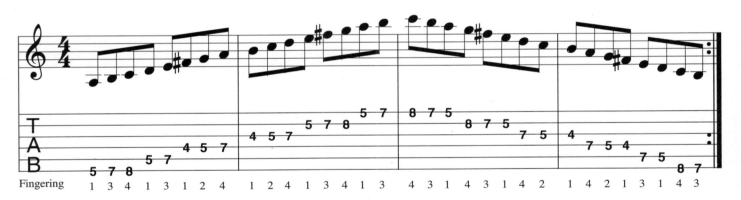

Fingering   1 3 4 1 3 1 2 4   1 2 4 1 3 4 1 3   4 3 1 4 3 1 4 2   1 4 2 1 3 1 4 3

28

This example shows the **A form** of **F Ionian**. The A form is identified by the root notes on the 5th and 3rd strings.

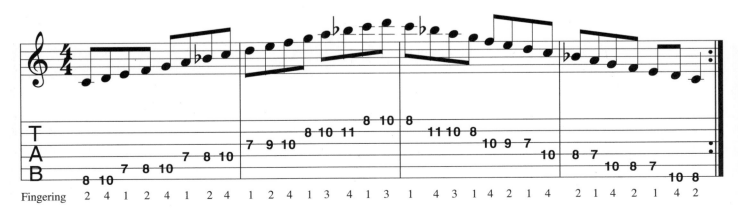

Fingering   2 4 1 2 4 1 2 4   1 2 4 1 3 4 1 3   1 4 3 1 4 2 1 4   2 1 4 2 1 4 2

Once you know the fingering for each scale form, practice each one using various sequence patterns as shown in the following examples. This first one uses the A form of C Ionian.

 29

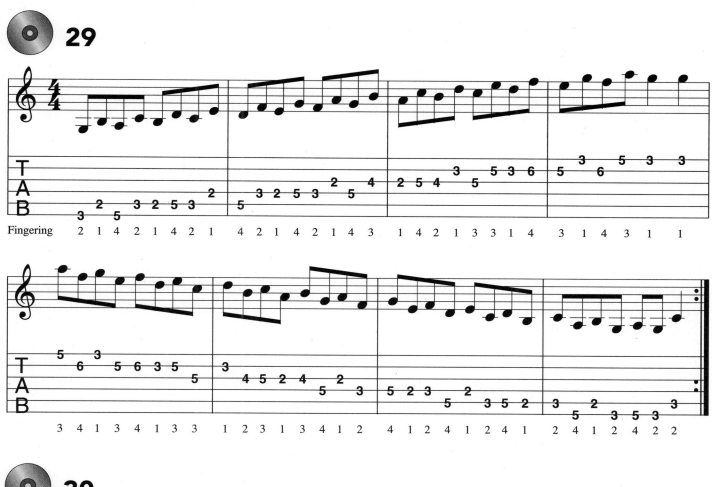

 30

The following example shows a 16th note sequence played in the G form of C Ionian.

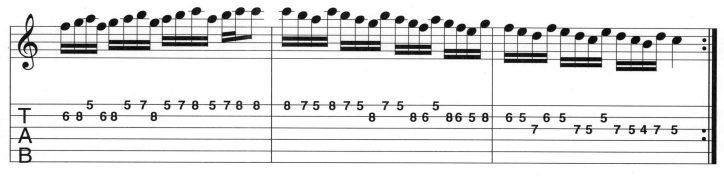

31

This example shows a triplet run using hammer-ons and pull-offs played in the D form of C Ionian.

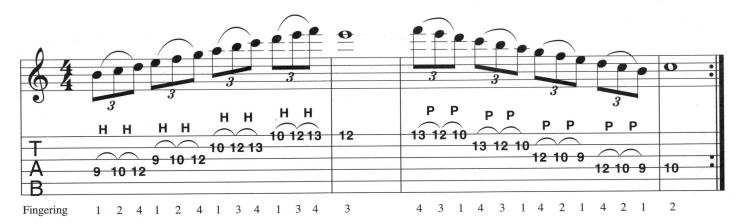

It is important to remember that scales are just the raw material for making music and are not an end in themselves. The purpose of learning all the forms and practicing sequence patterns is to become comfortable with them in order to make melodic statements. Once you are confident with the scale forms, exeriment with various techniques (e.g. bends, hammer-ons, slides, etc) and create some of your own licks and solos from them. The following example shows a lick derived from the G form of C Ionian. Try out your own ideas with the Ionian mode jam along progression on page 82.

32

Dorian Mode

Formula – 1 2 ♭3 4 5 6 ♭7

Like the Ionian mode, the Dorian mode can also be played in five different forms which cover the fretboard. The fingerings for the Dorian mode are the same as those of the Ionian mode, except that the root notes are in different position. Once again it is always the position of the root notes which determines the name of each form. The following examples show the five forms of **C Dorian**.

Open Position C Form

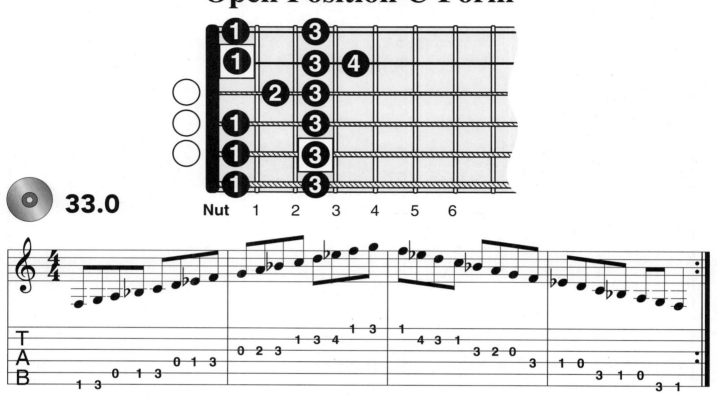

33.0

A Form

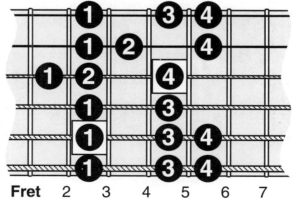

33.1

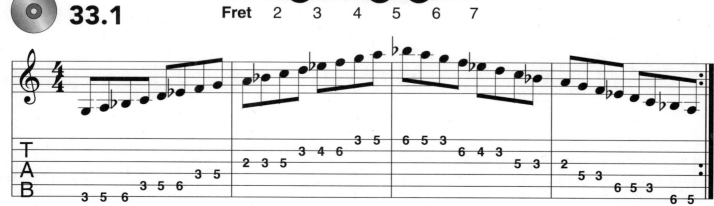

G Form

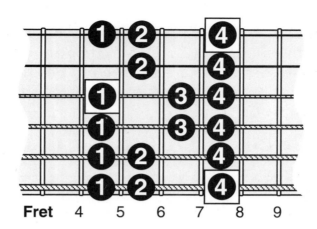

33.2

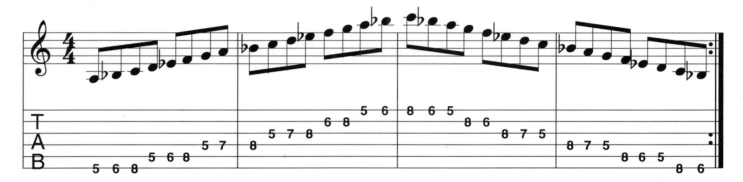

E Form

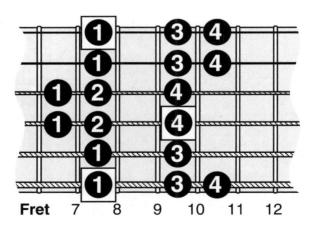

33.3

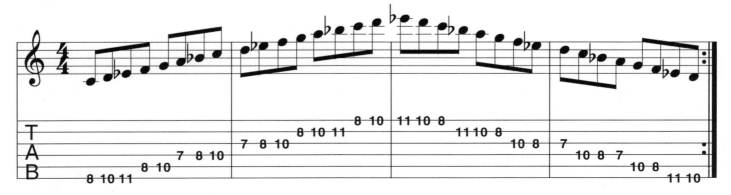

D Form

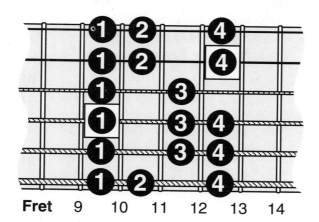

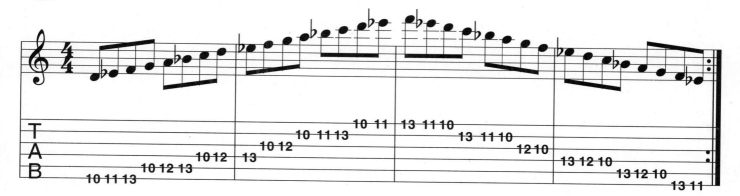

C Form

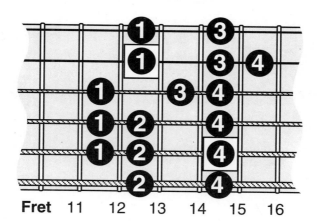

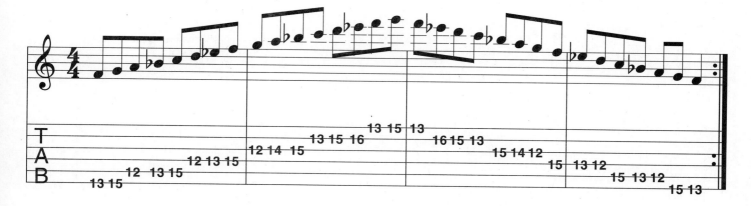

Licks Using the Dorian Mode

Once again, when you are comfortable with the fingerings for the Dorian mode, practice each form using intervals and sequences and then try creating your own licks. Written below are three licks derived from the C Dorian mode. Each lick is played over a minor seventh chord. The Dorian mode can also be used to play over minor, minor sixth and minor ninth chords. Try playing these licks along with some of your own against the Dorian jam along progression on page 82.

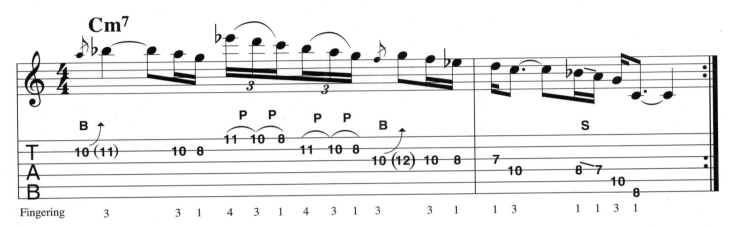

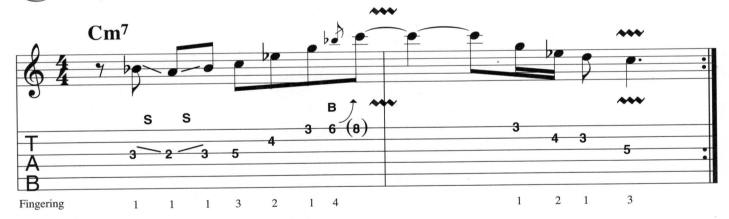

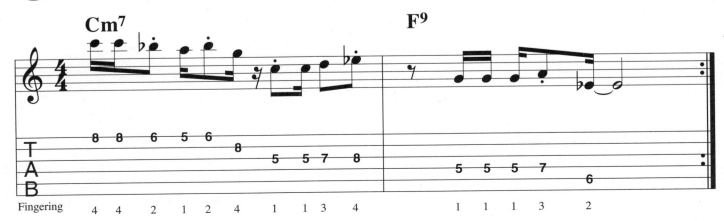

Phrygian Mode

Formula – 1 ♭2 ♭3 4 5 ♭6 ♭7

The following examples show the five forms of **C Phrygian**. Once again, the fingerings are the same but the root notes which determine the name of each form are in different positions.

Open Position C Form

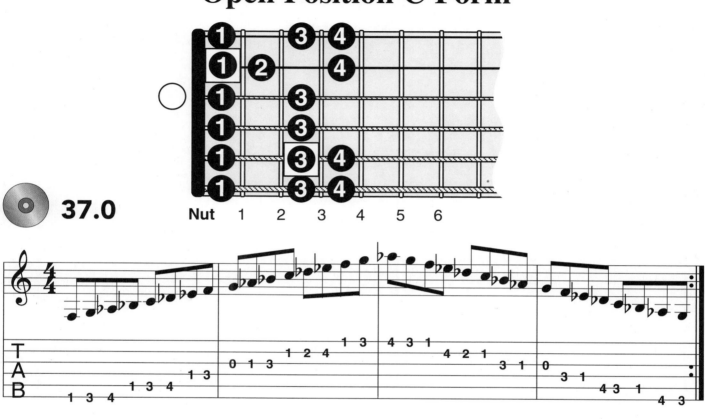

37.0

A Form

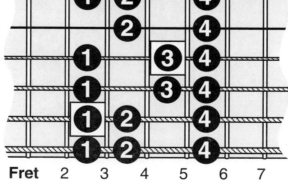

37.1

G Form

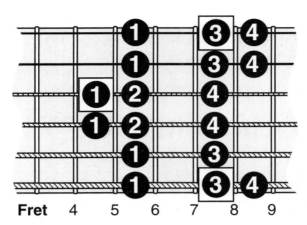

E Form

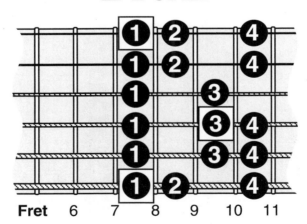

D Form

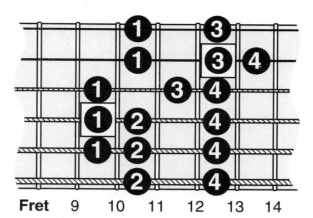

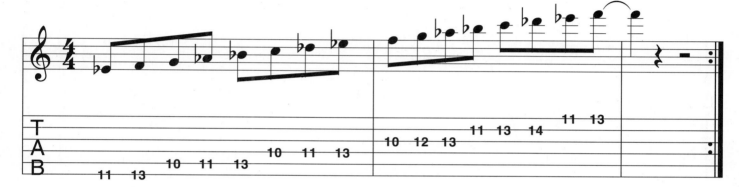

37.4

C Form

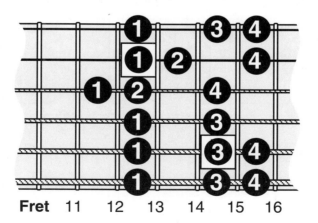

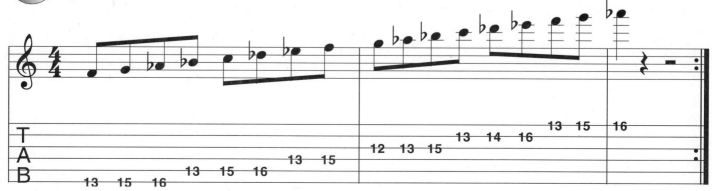

37.5

Licks Using the Phrygian Mode

Written below are three licks demonstrating some of the sounds available in the Phrygian mode. The Phrygian mode is commonly played over minor or minor seventh chords. Once you are comfortable with these licks, try playing them against the Phrygian jam along progression on page 82.

 38

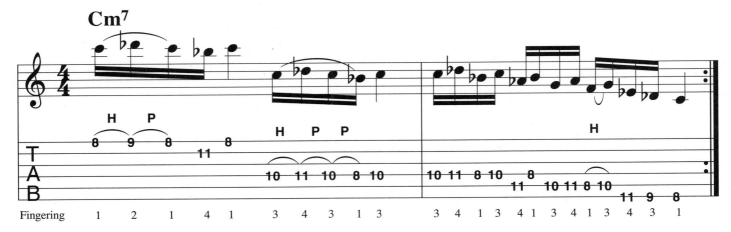

 39

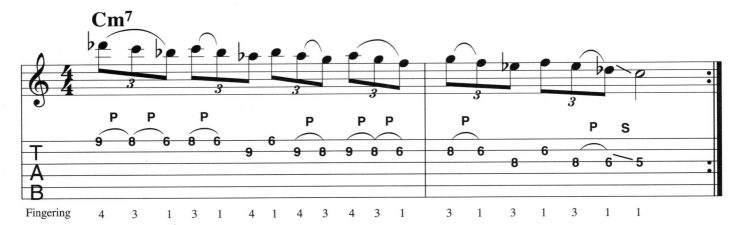

 **40**

Lydian Mode

Formula – 1 2 3 ♯4 5 6 7

The following examples show the five forms of **C Lydian**. Once again, the fingerings are the same but the root notes which determine the name of each form are in different positions.

Open Position C Form

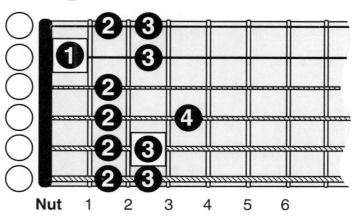

 **41.0**

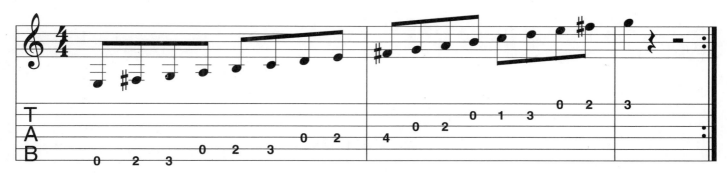

A Form

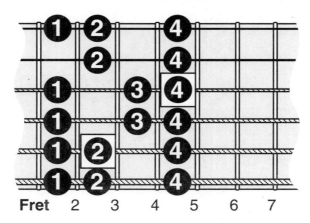

 **41.1**

G Form

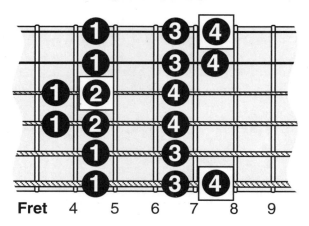

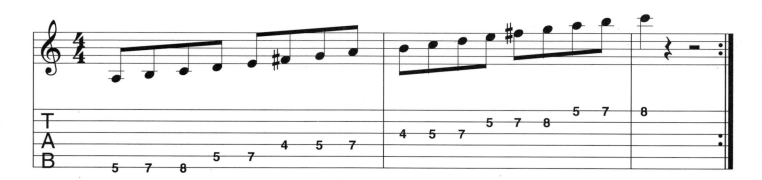

41.2

E Form

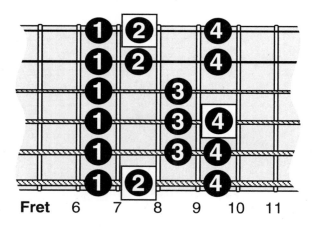

41.3

D Form

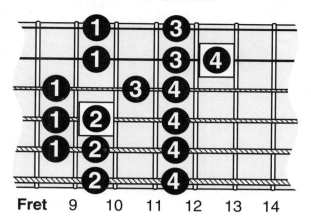

41.4

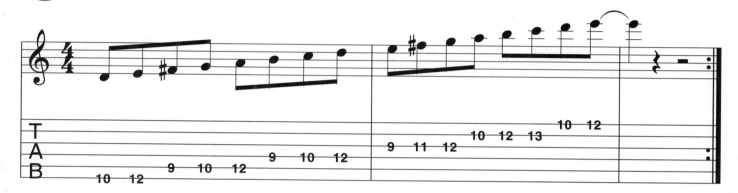

C Form

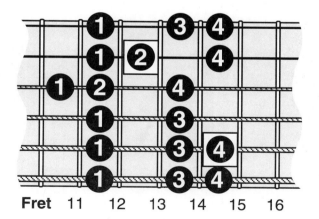

41.5

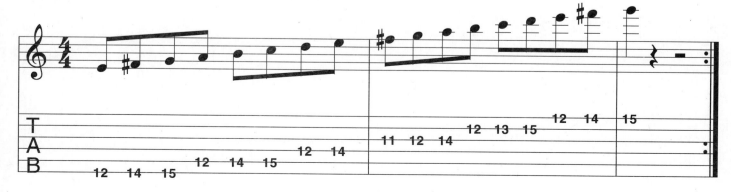

Licks Using the Lydian Mode

Written below are three licks demonstrating some of the sounds available in the Lydian mode. The Lydian mode is commonly played over major, major seventh and major ♯11 chords. Experiment with these licks and some of your own against the Lydian jam along progression on page 82.

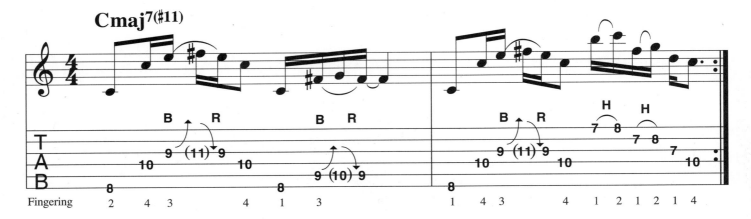

Mixolydian Mode

Formula – 1 2 3 4 5 6 ♭7

The following examples show the five forms of **C Mixolydian**. Once again, the fingerings are the same but the root notes which determine the name of each form are in different positions.

Open Position C Form

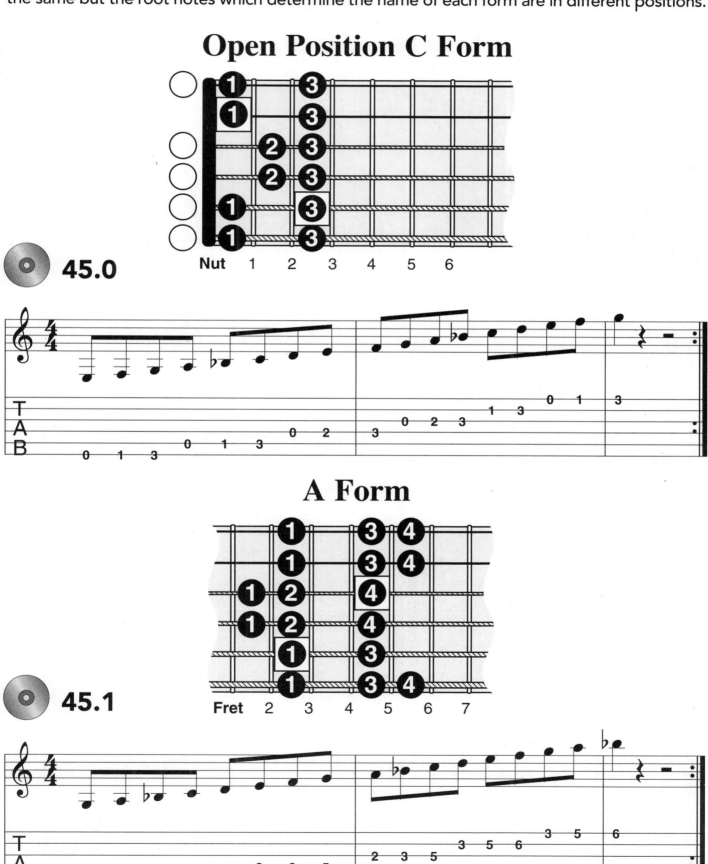

45.0

A Form

45.1

G Form

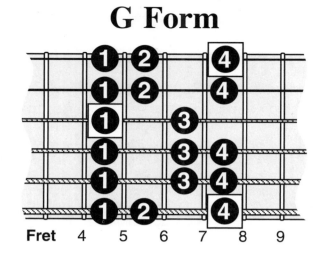

Fret 4 5 6 7 8 9

45.2

E Form

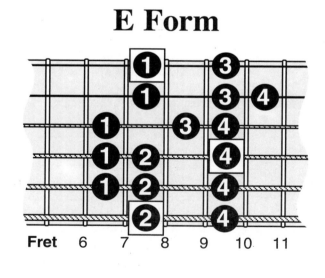

Fret 6 7 8 9 10 11

45.3

D Form

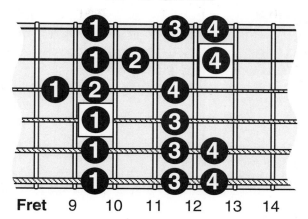

45.4

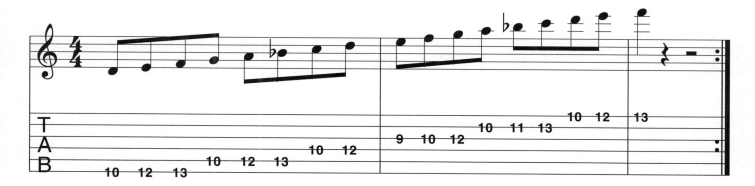

C Form

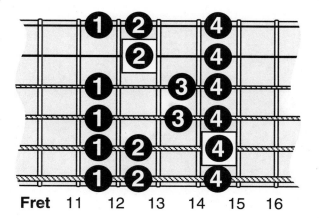

45.5

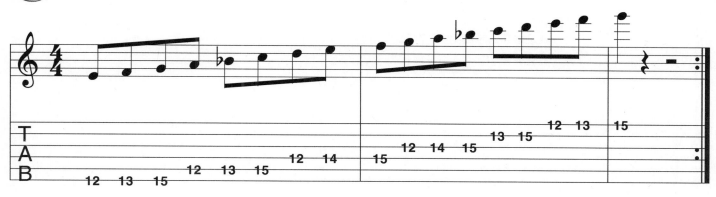

Licks Using the Mixolydian Mode

Written below are three licks demonstrating some of the sounds available in the Mixolydian mode. The Mixolydian mode is commonly played over dominant chords such as sevenths, ninths and thirteenths. As with previous modes, once you know these licks, try playing along with the Mixolydian jam along progression on page 82.

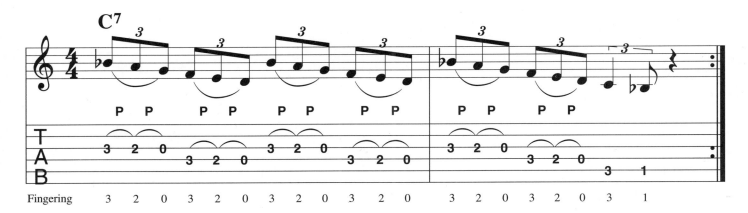

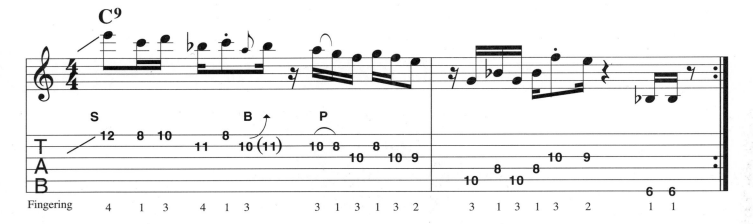

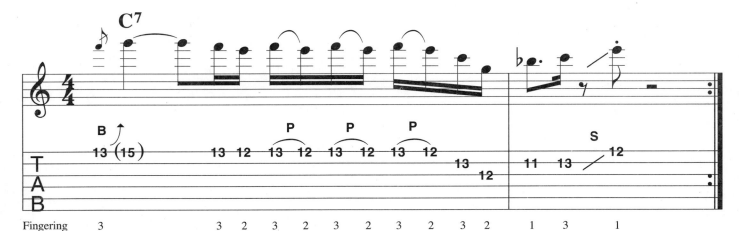

Aeolian Mode

Formula – 1 2 ♭3 4 5 ♭6 ♭7

The following examples show the five forms of **C Aeolian**. Once again, the fingerings are the same but the root notes which determine the name of each form are in different positions.

Open Position C Form

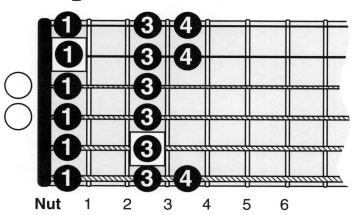

49.0

A Form

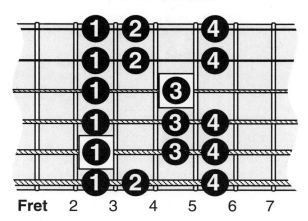

49.1

G Form

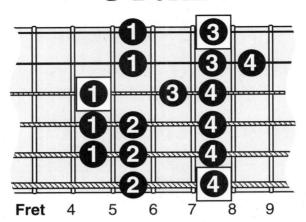

 **49.2**

E Form

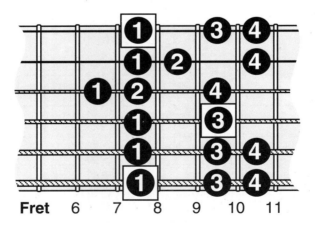

D Form

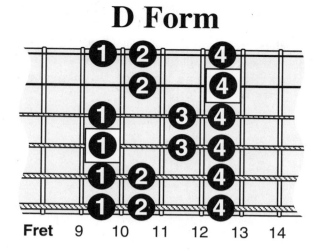

| Fret | 9 | 10 | 11 | 12 | 13 | 14 |

49.4

C Form

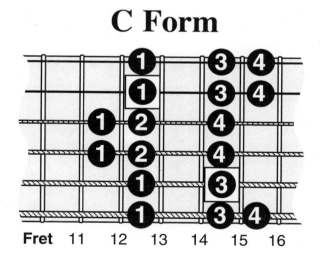

| Fret | 11 | 12 | 13 | 14 | 15 | 16 |

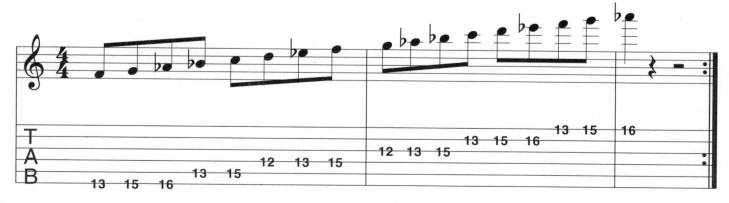

49.5

Licks Using the Aeolian Mode

The following licks demonstrate some of the sounds available in the Aeolian mode. The Aeolian mode is commonly played over minor, minor seventh and minor ninth chords. Once again, try using these licks and other ideas against the Aeolian jam along progression on page 83.

 50

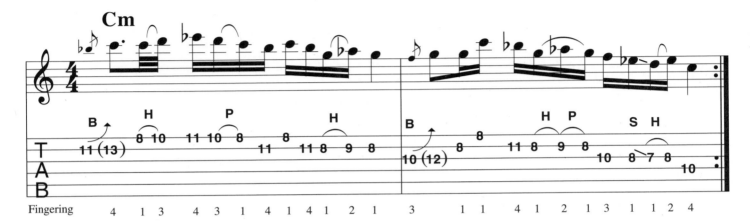

 **51**

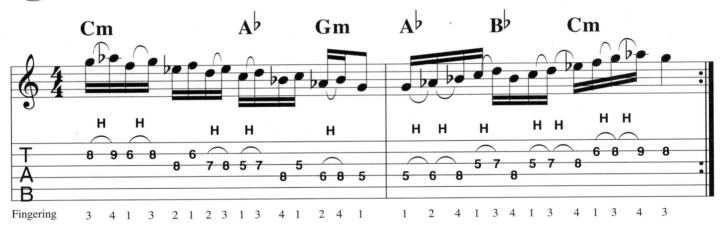

 **52**

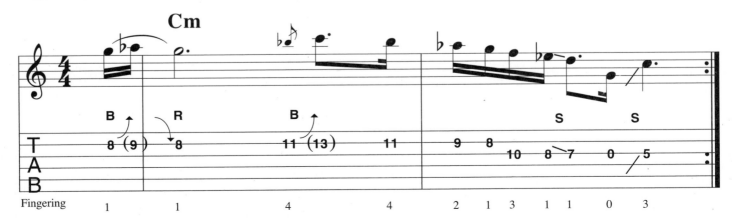

Locrian Mode

Formula – 1 ♭2 ♭3 4 ♭5 ♭6 ♭7

The following examples show the five forms of **C Locrian**. Once again, the fingerings are the same but the root notes which determine the name of each form are in different positions.

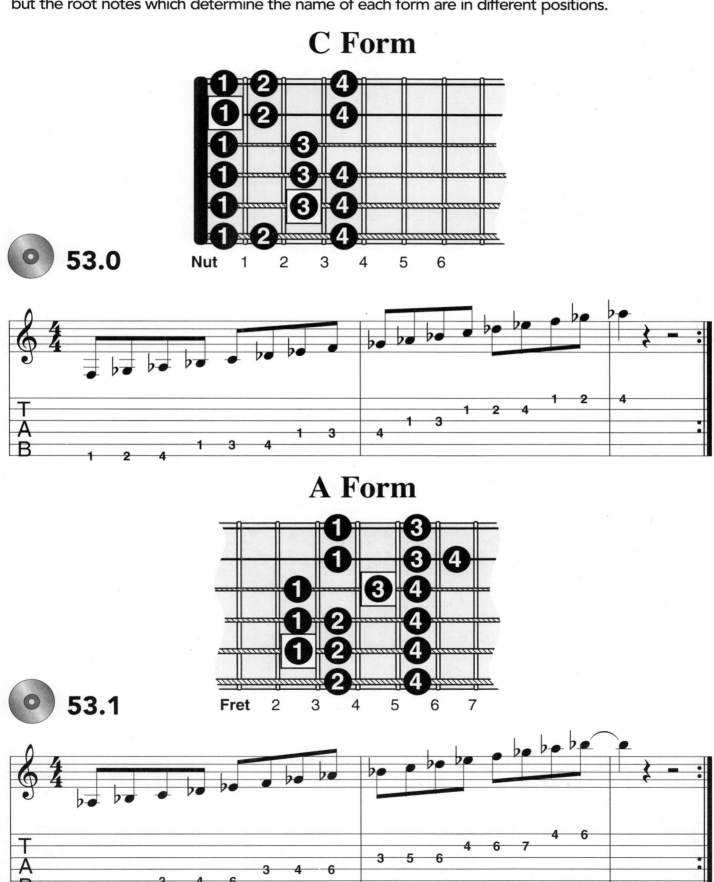

C Form

53.0

A Form

53.1

G Form

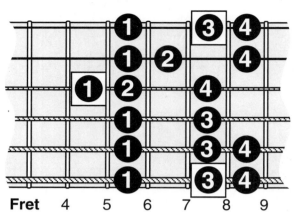

53.2

E Form

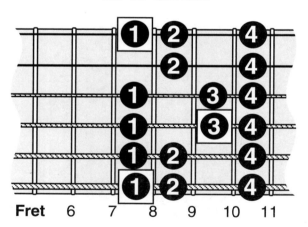

53.3

D Form

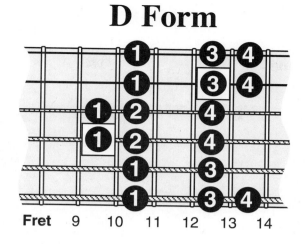

53.4

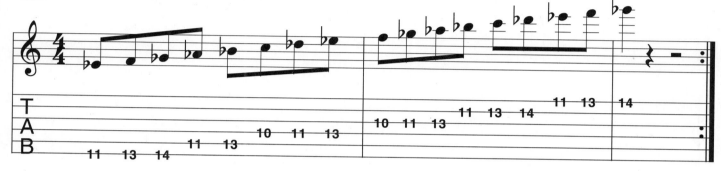

Licks Using the Locrian Mode

The following examples are licks derived from the C Locrian mode. The Locrian mode is most commonly played against minor seven flat five chords. Try using it with the Locrian jam along progression on page 83.

54

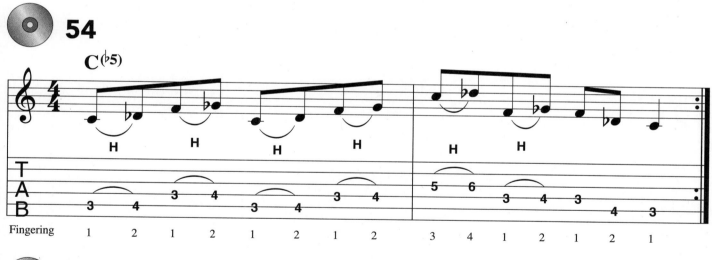

55

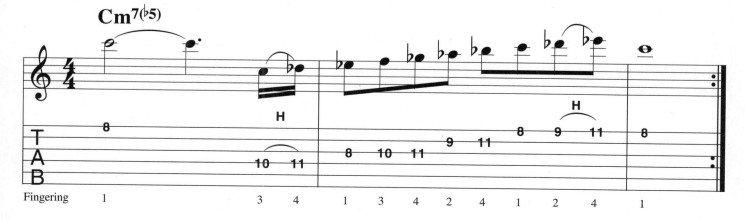

SECTION 3
Minor Scales

Harmonic Minor Scale

All of the modes you have learnt so far have been derived from the major scale, even if some of them have a minor sound. The **Aeolian** mode is also called the **natural minor scale** and can be played against many minor key chord progressions. There are two other important minor scales which are commonly used in many styles of music. These are the **harmonic minor** and the **melodic minor**. These two scales are dealt with in this section. First let's take a look at the harmonic minor scale. Written below is the **C harmonic minor scale** over one octave in the open position. Listen carefully to the sound of the scale as you play and try to memorise it. Learning any scale becomes easier once you have the sound of it in your memory.

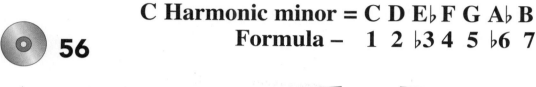

56

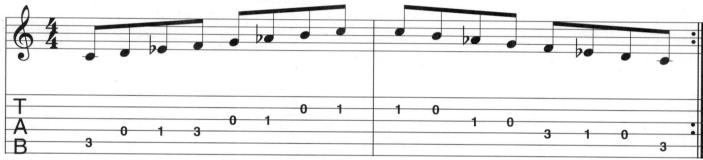

Harmonic Minor in Five Forms

Like the modes derived from the major scale, there are five forms of the harmonic minor scale which cover the fretboard when placed end to end.

Open Position C Form

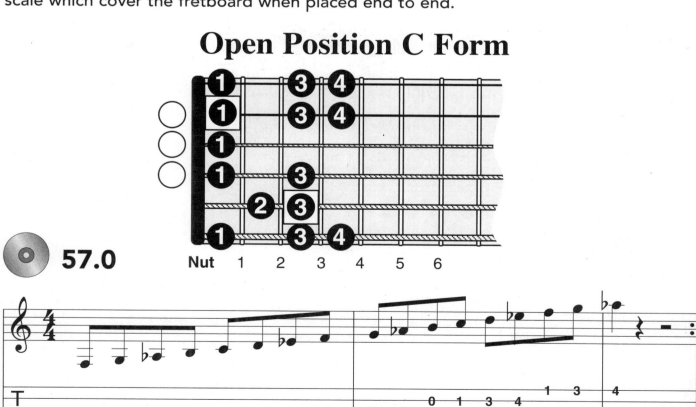

57.0

A Form

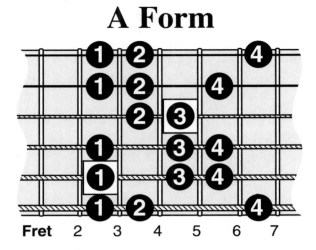

57.1

G Form

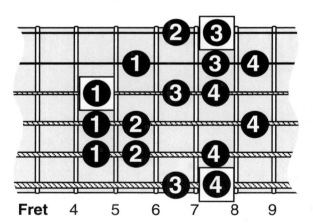

57.2

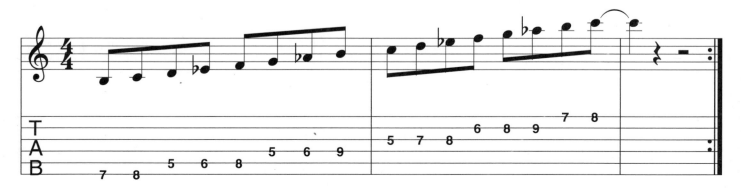

E Form

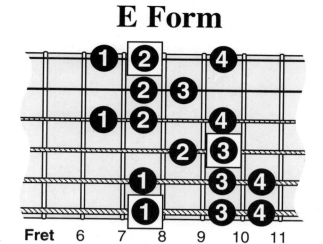

Fret 6 7 8 9 10 11

57.3

D Form

Fret 9 10 11 12 13 14

57.4

C Form

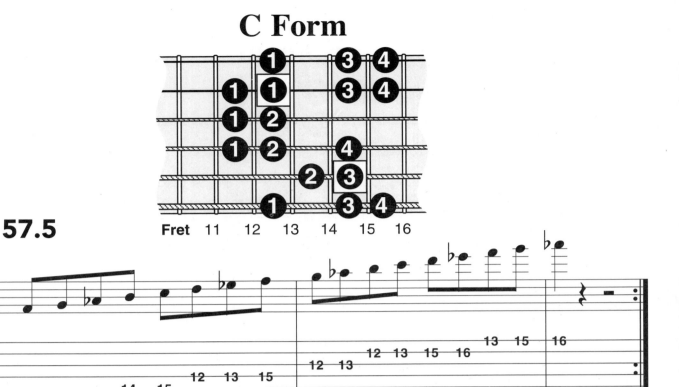

57.5

Licks Using the Harmonic Minor

The following examples are licks derived from the C harmonic minor scale. The harmonic minor is most commonly played against chord progressions in a minor key where chord V is a major or dominant chord. It is also commonly used against power chords (root and fifth only). Try using it with the Harmonic minor jam along progression on page 83.

58

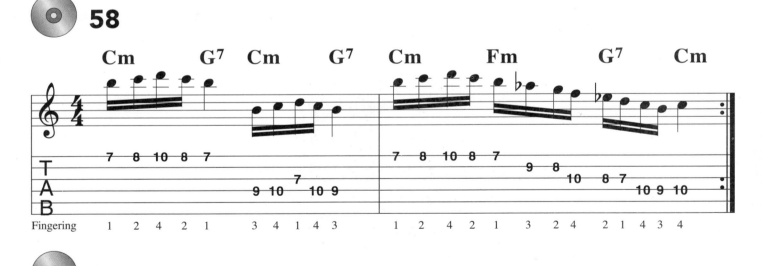

59

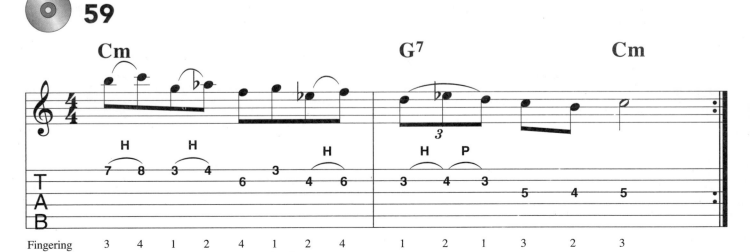

Melodic Minor Scale

The other important minor scale is the **melodic minor**. There are two versions of the melodic minor scale, one comes from Classical music and the other is commonly used in Jazz. The traditional Classical version of the melodic minor ascends with the degrees 1, 2, ♭3, 4, 5, 6, 7 and descends as the natural minor or Aeolian mode. The Jazz melodic minor descends with exactly the same degrees as it ascends. It is this second version which is dealt with here.

C Melodic minor = C D E♭ F G A B

Formula – 1 2 ♭3 4 5 6 7

60

This example shows one octave of the melodic minor scale in the open position. Once again, try to memorise the sound of the scale as well as the fingering.

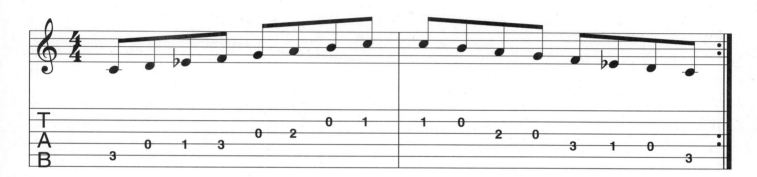

Melodic Minor in Five Forms

Open Position C Form

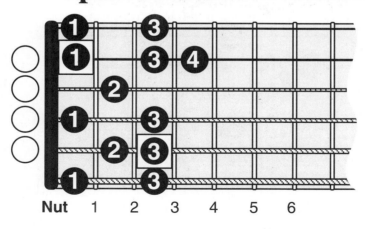

Nut   1   2   3   4   5   6

61.0

A Form

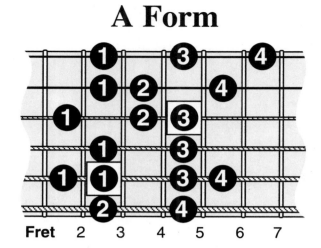

61.1

G Form

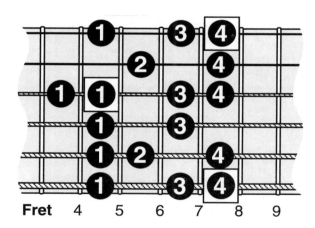

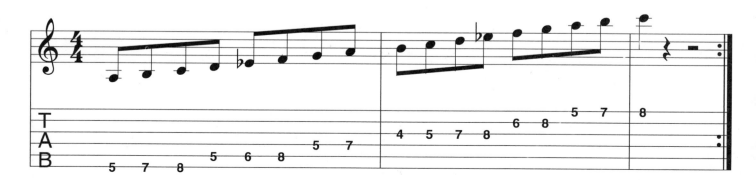

61.2

E Form

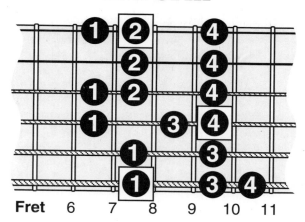

 **61.3**

D Form

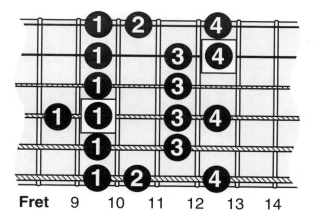

61.4

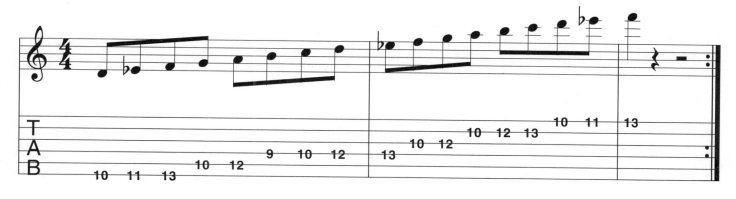

C Form

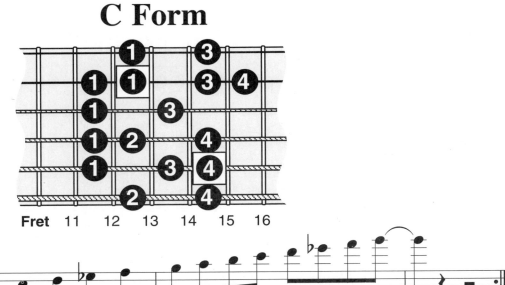

Fret 11 12 13 14 15 16

61.5

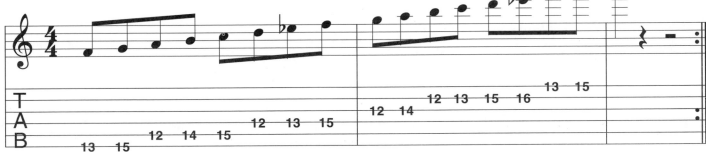

Licks Using the Melodic Minor

Here are two licks which use the C melodic minor scale. The melodic minor can be used in many different ways, both against minor key progressions and dominant chords. Try playing these licks along with some of your own against the Melodic minor jam along progression on page 83. (For more on the melodic minor and its uses, see *Progressive Jazz Lead Guitar Technique*).

62

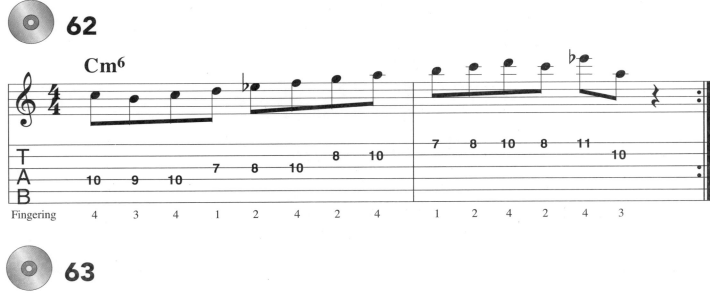

63

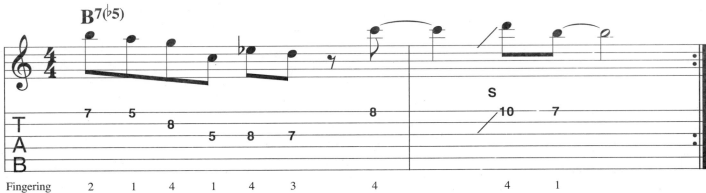

SECTION 4
Other Useful Scales

Minor Pentatonic Scale

The **minor pentatonic scale** is probably the most common scale used in lead guitar playing. It contains only **five** different notes and has a "Bluesy" kind of sound. The C minor pentatonic scale is shown below in the open position.

C Minor Pentatonic = C E♭ F G B♭

Formula – 1 ♭3 4 5 ♭7

Minor Pentatonic in Five Forms

Open Position C Form

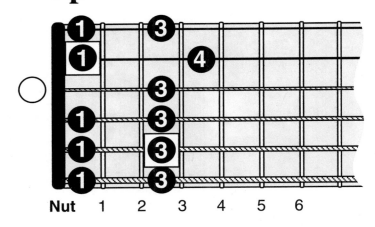

A Form

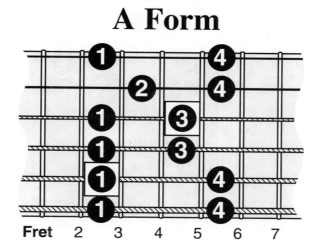

65.1

G Form

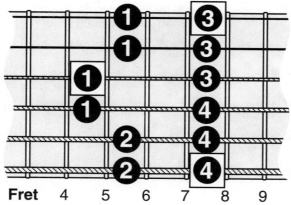

65.2

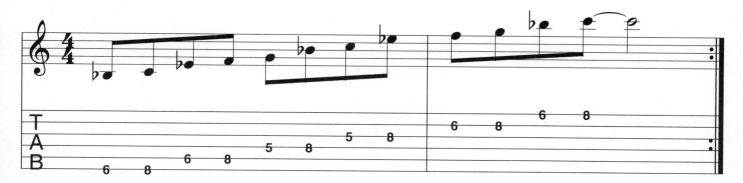

68

E Form

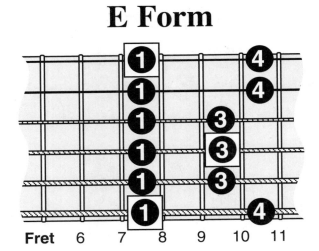

65.3

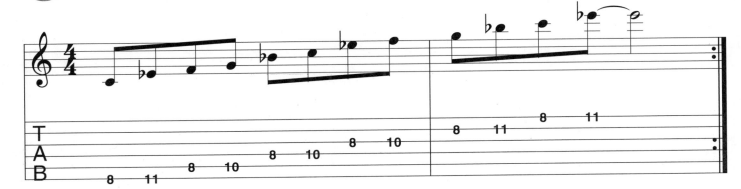

D Form

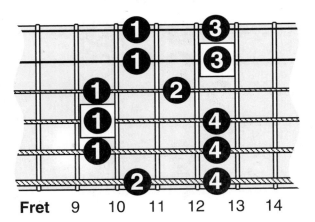

65.4

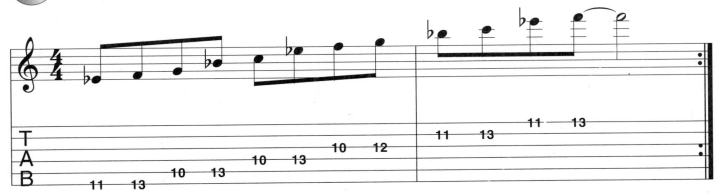

C Form

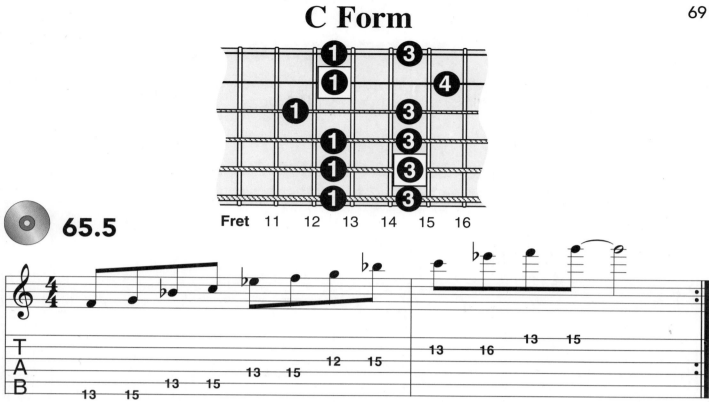

65.5

Licks Using the Minor Pentatonic

Here are two licks which use the C minor pentatonic scale. This scale sounds great with note bending. It can be used against a variety of minor key progressions, Blues progressions and major key Rock progressions. Try using the minor pentatonic against the jam along progressions at the end of the book, you'll find it will work against quite a few of them. (For more on the minor pentatonic and its uses, see *Progressive Blues Lead Guitar Method*).

66

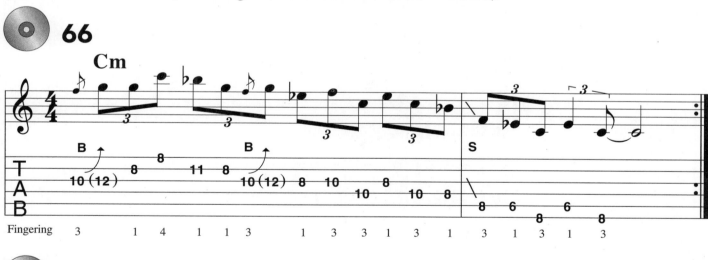

67

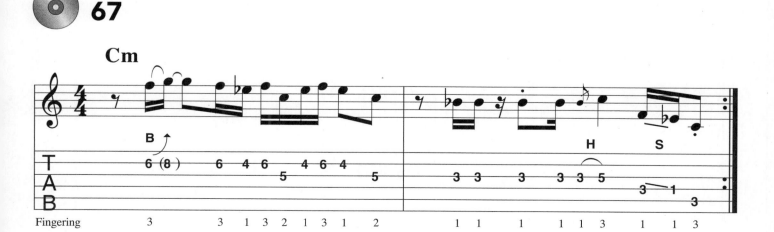

Blues Scale

The **Blues scale** is very similar to the minor pentatonic scale. The only difference is the added flattened fifth degree as shown in the formula below. The C Blues scale is shown below in the open position.

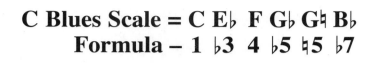

C Blues Scale = C E♭ F G♭ G♮ B♭
Formula – 1 ♭3 4 ♭5 ♮5 ♭7

68

Blues Scale in Five Forms

Open Position C Form

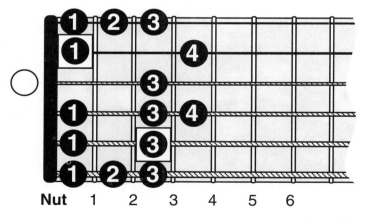

Nut 1 2 3 4 5 6

69.0

A Form

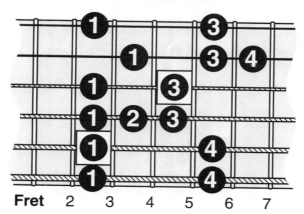

69.1

G Form

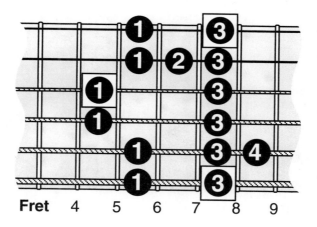

69.2

E Form

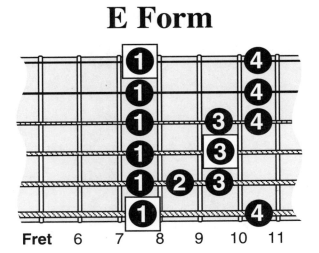

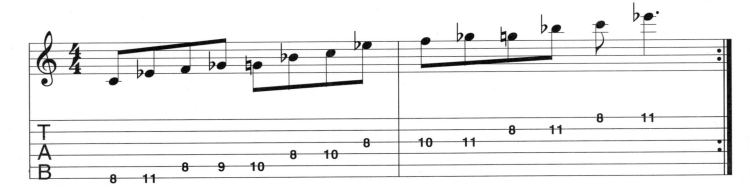

D Form

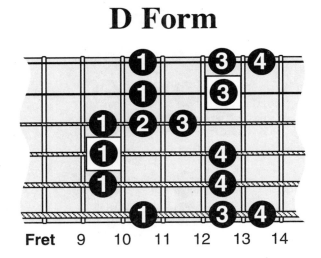

C Form

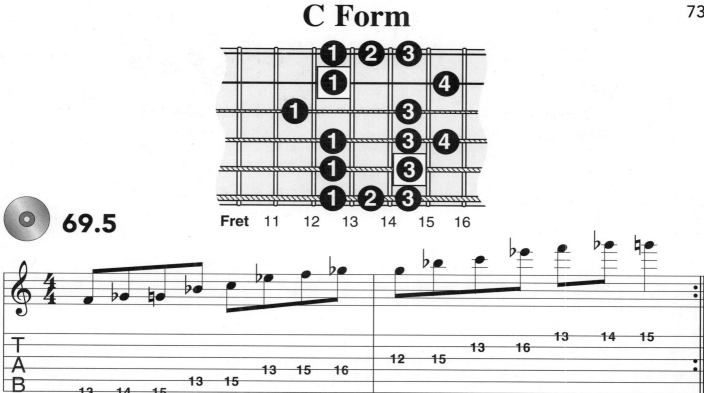

69.5

Licks Using the Blues Scale

Here are two licks which use the C Blues scale. Like the minor pentatonic, the Blues scale can be used against minor key progressions, Blues progressions and major key Rock progressions. Try using it against the jam along progressions at the end of the book. (For more on the Blues scale and its uses, see *Progressive Blues Lead Guitar Technique*).

70

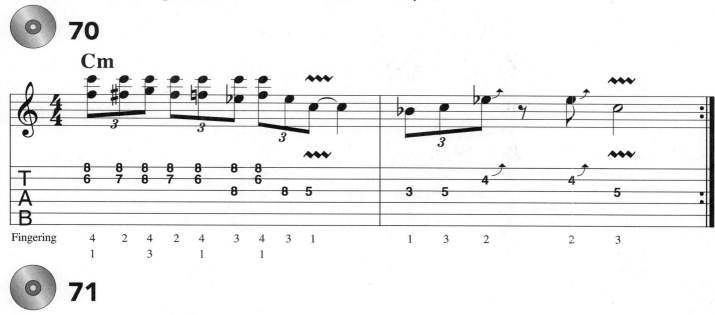

71

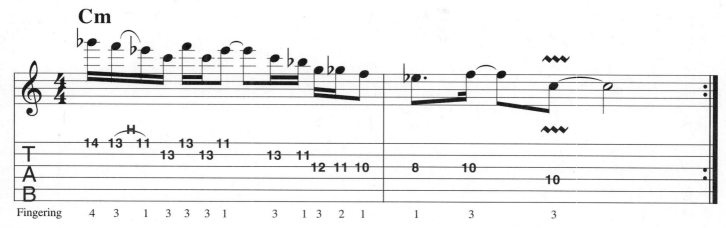

Major Pentatonic Scale

The **major pentatonic scale** is another particularly useful scale for improvising. Like the minor pentatonic it contains only five different notes, but has a much more major sound. The C major pentatonic scale is shown below in the open position.

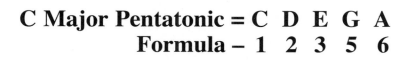

C Major Pentatonic = C D E G A
Formula – 1 2 3 5 6

72

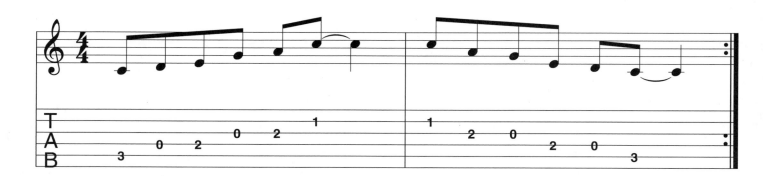

Major Pentatonic in Five Forms

Open Position C Form

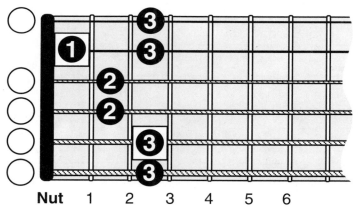

Nut   1   2   3   4   5   6

73.0

A Form

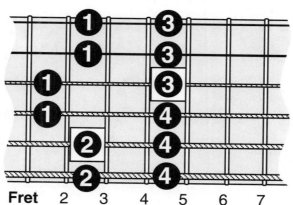

73.1

G Form

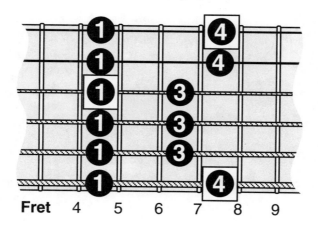

73.2

E Form

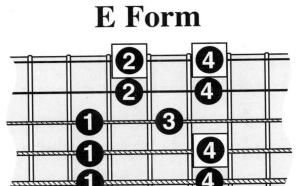

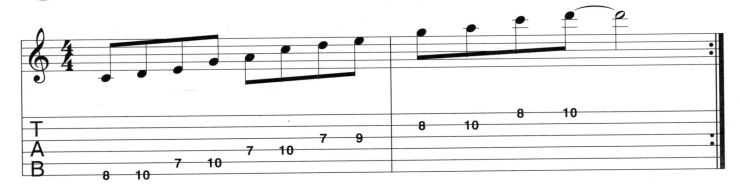

73.3

D Form

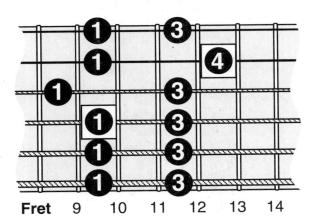

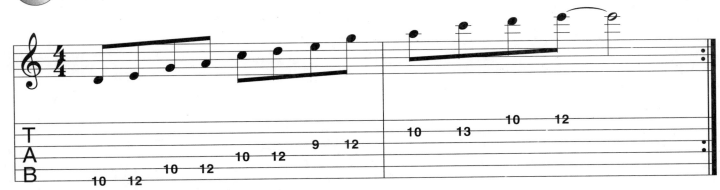

73.4

C Form

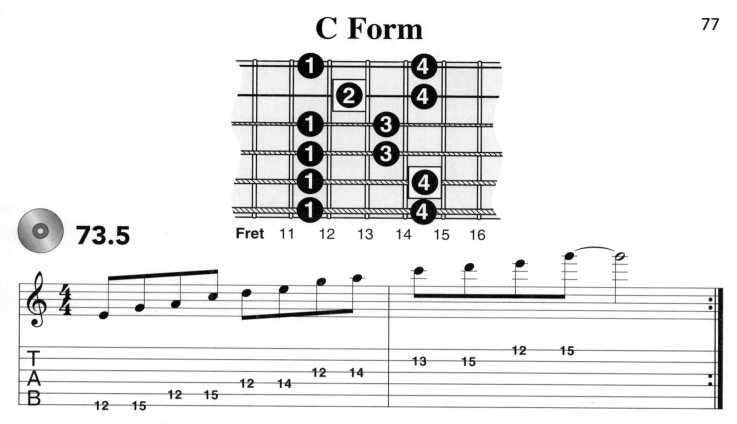

73.5

Licks Using the Major Pentatonic

Here are two licks which use the C major pentatonic scale. This scale is also useful in a variety of situations and can be used over many chord progressions, including major key progressions and Blues progressions. Once again, try using it against some of the jam along progressions at the end of the book. (For more on the major pentatonic scale and its uses, see *Progressive Blues Lead Guitar Technique*).

74

75

Whole Tone Scale

The **whole tone scale** is another useful scale, particularly for playing over augmented chords and dominant chords with a raised 5th. The whole tone scale contains **six** different notes and is made up entirely of major second intervals. The C whole tone scale is shown below in the open position. As with previous scales, play it several times until you have the sound memorised.

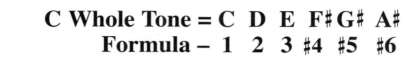

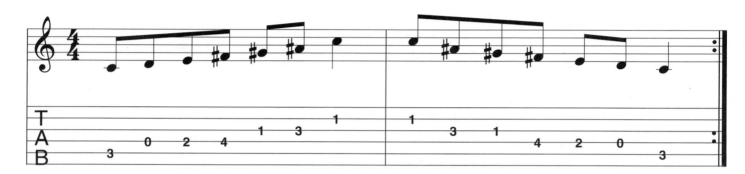

Moveable fingerings

Because the whole tone scale is a symmetrical scale which does not follow major or minor chord shapes, it does not follow the five forms like previous scales. Here are two useful moveable fingerings of the whole tone scale.

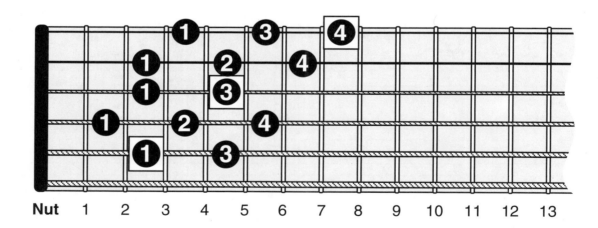

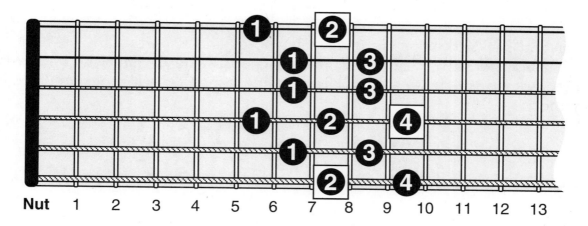

 **77.1**

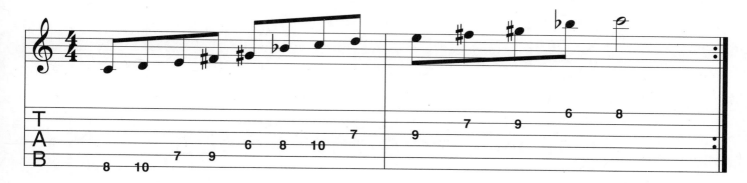

Here is a lick derived from the C whole tone scale. As you can hear, it's a colorful sound. Experiment with this scale and create some of your own licks against the Whole Tone scale jam along progression on page 84.

78

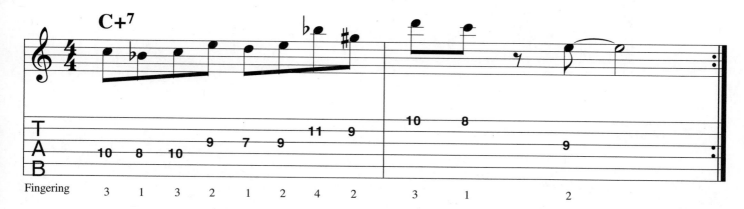

Diminished Scale

The **diminished scale** contains **eight** different notes and is particularly useful for playing over diminished chords and altered dominant chords. The C diminished scale is shown below in the open position. As with previous scales, play it several times until you have the sound memorised.

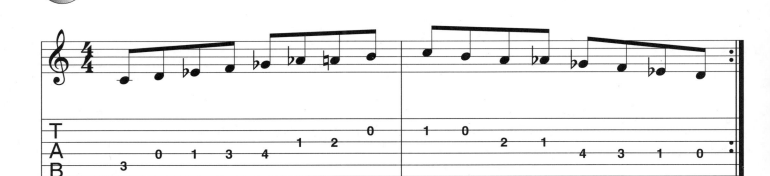

Moveable fingerings

Like the whole tone scale, the diminished scale does not follow the five forms like the earlier scales. Here are two useful moveable fingerings of the diminished scale.

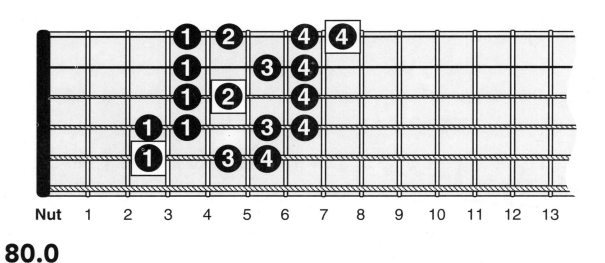

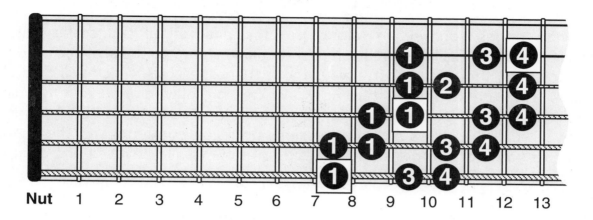

 **80.1**

Here is a lick derived from the C diminished scale. This scale may sound strange at first, but it is well worth learning and can produce some very interesting sounds. Try using it against the Diminished scale jam along progression on page 84.

81

Jam along Progressions

The following pages contain jam along progressions for all the scales and modes presented in the book. Each progression is particularly suited to the scale or mode written above it. However, there is almost always more than one scale which will fit a chord or progression. E.g. the minor pentatonic scale can be played against any minor key progression as well as Dorian, Phrygian and Blues progressions among other things. Experiment with all the scales and progressions until you come up with the sounds that sound right to you. For a more detialed study of how to play over chord changes, see *Progressive Jazz Lead Guitar Method*.

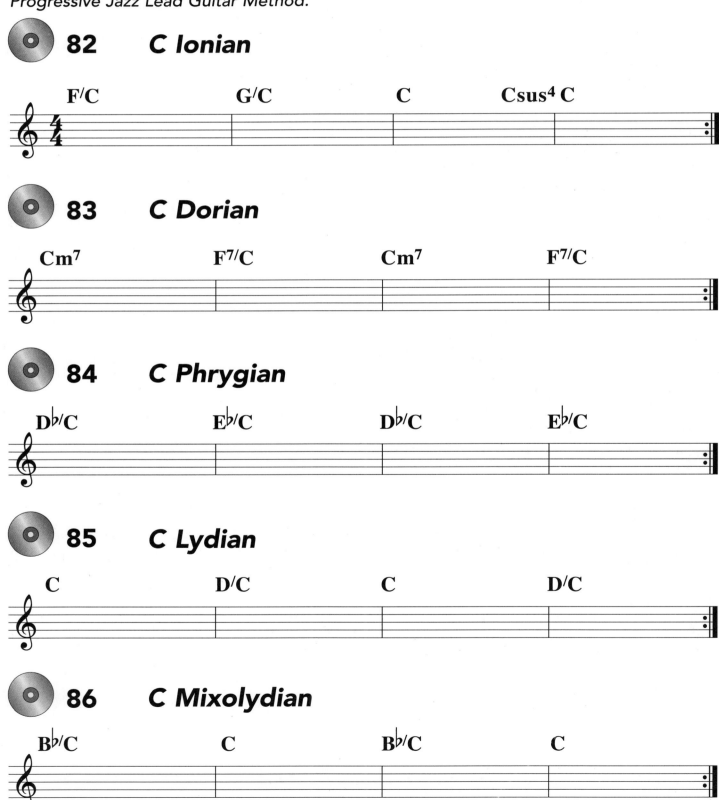

82 *C Ionian*

| F/C | G/C | C | Csus^4 C |

83 *C Dorian*

| Cm^7 | F^7/C | Cm^7 | F^7/C |

84 *C Phrygian*

| D$^\flat$/C | E$^\flat$/C | D$^\flat$/C | E$^\flat$/C |

85 *C Lydian*

| C | D/C | C | D/C |

86 *C Mixolydian*

| B$^\flat$/C | C | B$^\flat$/C | C |

87 *C Aeolian*

A♭/C	B♭/C	A♭/C	B♭/C

88 *C Locrian*

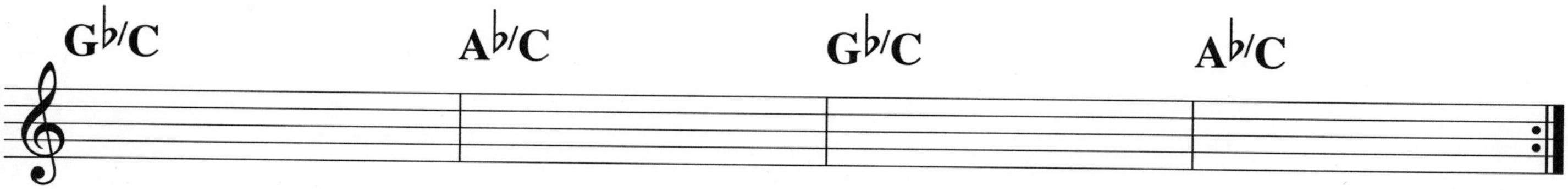

G♭/C	A♭/C	G♭/C	A♭/C

89 *C Major/Aminor Progression*

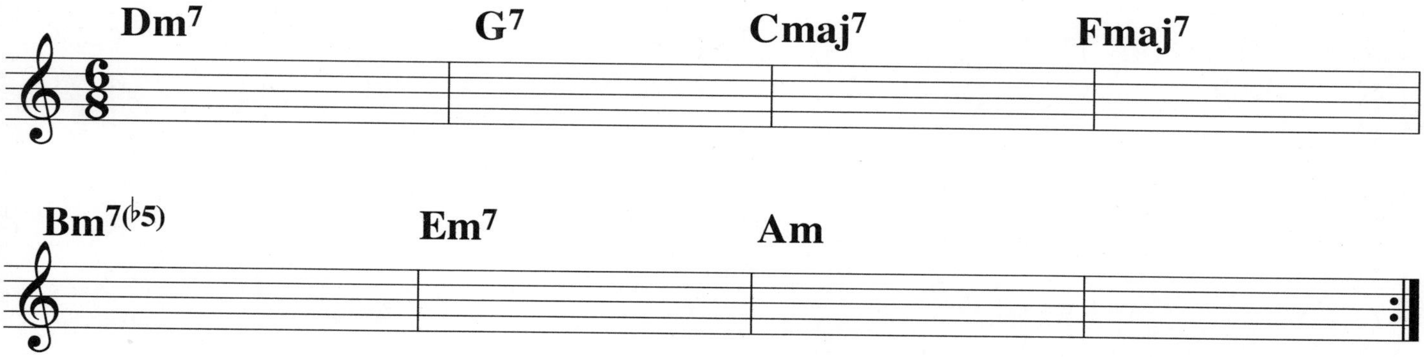

Dm⁷	G⁷	Cmaj⁷	Fmaj⁷

Bm⁷⁽♭⁵⁾	Em⁷	Am	

90 *C Natural Minor*

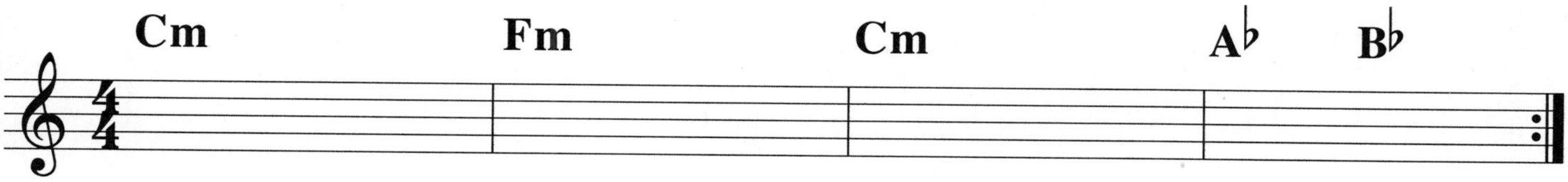

Cm	Fm	Cm	A♭ B♭

91 *C Harmonic Minor*

Cm	G⁷	Fm	G⁷

92 *C Melodic Minor*

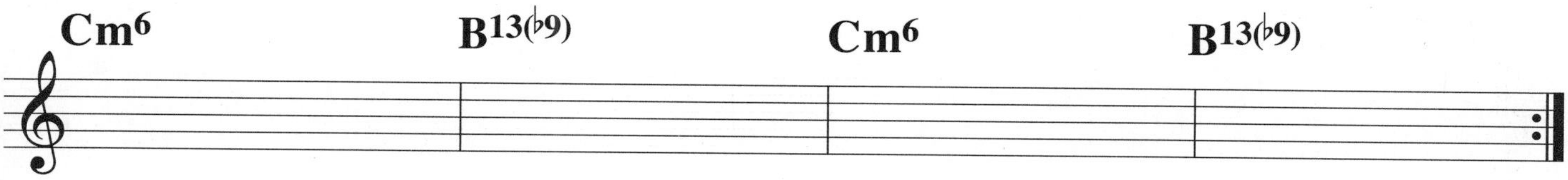

Cm⁶	B¹³⁽♭⁹⁾	Cm⁶	B¹³⁽♭⁹⁾

93 ***12 Bar Blues in C***

There are many scales and modes which can be played against Blues progressions, the most common being the minor and major pentatonic scales and the Blues scale. Other common scales used in Blues are the Dorian and Mixolydian modes. In Jazz, there are many variations on the 12 bar Blues progression and almost any scale or mode can be used against it in the right situation. (For more on playing against Blues progressions, see *Progressive Blues Lead Guitar Method*, and *Progressive Blues Lead Guitar Technique*.)

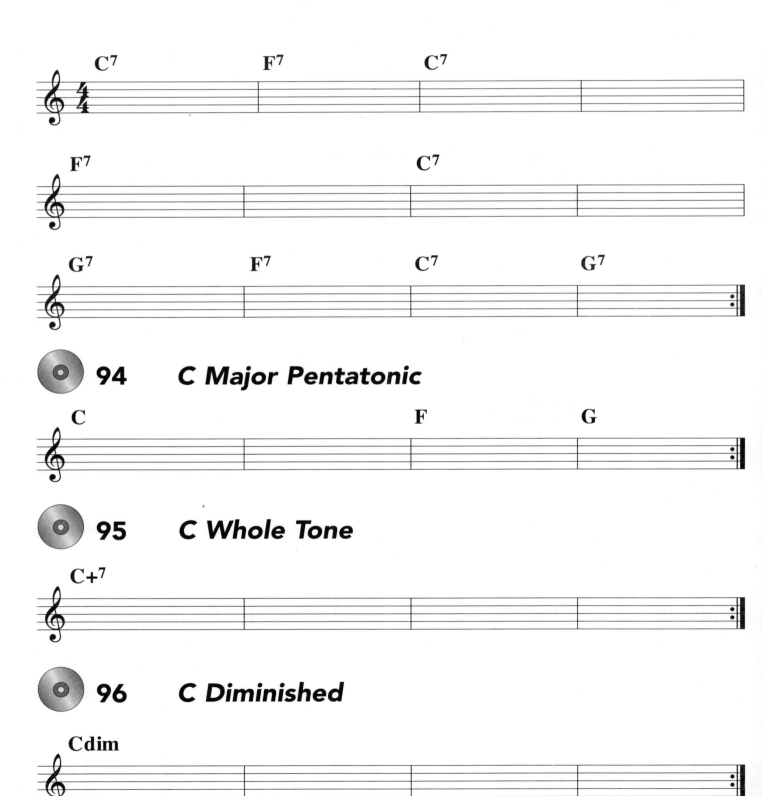

 94 ***C Major Pentatonic***

 95 ***C Whole Tone***

 96 ***C Diminished***

Learning the Keys

The term "**key**" describes the central note around which a piece of music is based, e.g. a piece of music in the key of **C** would derive its notes and chords from a **C major scale**. A piece of music in the key of **A** would derive its notes and chords from the **A major scale**, and so on. After you have learnt a scale or mode in one key, it is a good idea to practice playing in every key. **E** and **A** are fairly common keys for guitar, but if you are playing with a singer, you would have to play in whatever key suits their particualar voice. That could be **F♯** or **D♭** for example. Piano players tend to like the keys of **C**, **F** and **G**, and horn players like flat keys such as **F**, **B♭** and **E♭**. So, you can see there are good reasons for learning to play equally well in every key.

A good way to learn to play in all keys is to use the **key cycle** (also called the cycle of 5ths or cycle of 4ths). It contains the names of all the keys and is fairly easy to memorise.

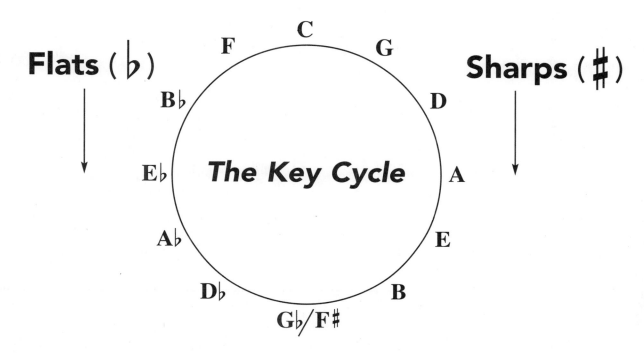

Think of the key cycle like a clock. Just as there are 12 points on the clock, there are also 12 keys. **C** is at the top and it contains no sharps or flats. Moving around clockwise you will find the next key is **G**, which contains one sharp (**F♯**). The next key is **D**, which contains two sharps (**F♯** and **C♯**). Progressing further through the sharp keys each key contains an extra sharp, with the new sharp being the 7th note of the new key, the other sharps being any which were contained in the previous key. Therefore the key of A would automatically contain F♯ and C♯ which were in the key of D, plus G♯ which is the 7th note of the A major scale. As you progress around the cycle, each key introduces a new sharp. When you get to F♯ (at 6 oclock), the new sharp is called E♯ which is enharmonically the same as **F**. **Enharmonic** means two different ways of writing the same note. Another example of enharmonic spelling would be F♯ and G♭. This means that G♭ could become the name of the key of F♯. The key of F♯ contains six sharps, while the key of G♭ contains six flats.

If you start at **C** again at the top of the cycle and go anti-clockwise you will progress through the flat keys. The key of **F** contains one flat (**B♭**), which then becomes the name of the next key around the cycle. In flat keys, the new flat is always the 4th degree of the new key. Continuing around the cycle, the key of **B♭** contains two flats (**B♭** and **E♭**) and so on.

Written below are the key signatures for all the major scales that contain sharps.

Sharps F#   F#C#   F#C#G#   F#C#G#D#   F#C#G#D#A#   F#C#G#D#A#E#

The sharp key signatures are summarised in the table below.

	Key	Number of Sharps	Sharp Notes
*The new sharp **key** is a fifth interval higher*	G	1	F#
	D	2	F#, C#
	A	3	F#, C#, G#
	E	4	F#, C#, G#, D#
	B	5	F#, C#, G#, D#, A#,
	F#	6	F#, C#, G#, D#, A#, E#

*The new sharp **note** is a fifth interval higher*

Written below are the key signatures for all the major scales that contain flats.

Flats B♭   B♭E♭   B♭E♭A♭   B♭E♭A♭D♭   B♭E♭A♭D♭G♭   B♭E♭A♭D♭G♭C♭

The flat key signatures are summarised in the table below.

	Key	Number of Flats	Flat Notes
*The new flat **key** is a fourth interval higher*	F	1	B♭
	B♭	2	B♭, E♭
	E♭	3	B♭, E♭, A♭
	A♭	4	B♭, E♭, A♭, D♭
	D♭	5	B♭, E♭, A♭, D♭, G♭,
	G♭	6	B♭, E♭, A♭, D♭, G♭, C♭

*The new flat **note** is a fourth interval higher*

* For more information about keys, scales, intervals and music theory in general, see *Progressive Music Theory*.

Relative Keys

if you compare the **A natural minor** minor scale with the **C major** scale you will notice that they contain the same notes (except starting on a different note). Because of this, these two scales are referred to as "relatives"; **A minor** is the relative minor of **C major** and vice versa.

Major Scale: C Major   **Relative Minor Scale: A Minor (natural)**

The harmonic and melodic minor scale variations are also relatives of the same major scale, e.g. **A harmonic** and **A melodic minor** are relatives of **C major**. For every major scale (and ever major chord) there is a relative minor scale which is based upon the **6th note** of the major scale. This is outlined in the table below.

MAJOR KEY (I)	C	D#	D	E♭	E	F	F	G♭	G	A♭	A	B♭	B
RELATIVE MINOR KEY (VI)	Am	B♭m	Bm	Cm	C#m	Dm	D#m	E♭m	Em	Fm	F#m	Gm	G#m

Both the major and the relative minor share the same key signature, as illustrated in the examples below:

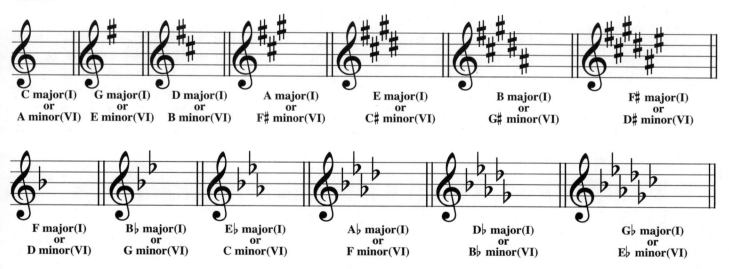

The sharpened **7th** note that occurs in the relative minor key is never included as part of the key signature. Because each major and relative minor share the same key signature, you will need to know how to distinguish between the two keys. For example, if given a piece with the key signature of **F#** thus:

It could indicate either the **key of G major** or its relative, **E minor**. The most accurate way of determining the key is to look through the melody for the sharpened **7th** note of the **E minor** scale (**D#**). The presence of this note will indicate the minor key. If the **7th** note is present, but not sharpened, then the key is more likely to be the relative major (i.e. **D** natural notes would suggest the **key of G major**).

Another method is to look at the first and last chords of the progression. These chords usually (but not always) indicate the key of the piece. If the piece starts and/or finishes with **Em** chords then the key is more likely to be **E minor**.

PROGRESSIVE JAZZ LEAD GUITAR METHOD
FOR BEGINNER TO INTERMEDIATE

A great introduction to Jazz lead guitar playing. Demonstrates all the essential rhythms, scales, modes and arpeggios needed to become a confident Jazz player. Also deals with playing over chord changes, understanding Swing and various approaches to improvisation.

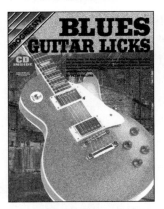

PROGRESSIVE BLUES GUITAR LICKS
FOR BEGINNER TO ADVANCED

Packed full of Blues guitar licks and solos incorporating styles and techniques used by the world's greatest Blues players. Includes sections on turnarounds, intro's and endings, call and response, dynamics and learning from other instruments. The licks cover a variety of styles such as shuffles, traditional slow Blues, Boogie, Jazz style Blues and R&B and Funk grooves. Also includes examples demonstrating how different licks can be put together to form whole solos, opening up endless possibilities for improvisation.

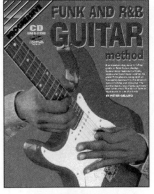

PROGRESSIVE FUNK AND R&B GUITAR METHOD
FOR BEGINNER TO ADVANCED

This book demonstrates many of the classic Funk sounds, using both rhythm and lead playing, since a good Funk player needs to be equally comfortable with both. A variety of chord forms are introduced within a framework that quickly allows the student to play confidently over the entire fretboard. Features an innovative approach to learning rhythms and applying them to riffs and grooves.

PROGRESSIVE ROCK GUITAR LICKS
FOR INTERMEDIATE TO ADVANCED

This book may be used by itself or as a useful supplement to *Progressive Rock Guitar Technique*. The licks throughout the book are examples of how the most popular lead guitar patterns can be used in all positions on the fretboard, and how various techniques can be applied to each pattern. Several Rock guitar solos are included to fully show how the licks and techniques studied throughout the book can be used to create a solo.

PROGRESSIVE GUITAR CHORDS
FOR BEGINNER TO ADVANCED GUITARISTS

Shows you every useful chord shape in every key. An open chord section for beginners contains the simplest and most widely used chord shapes in all keys. A bar chord section for the semi-advanced player who will need a thorough knowledge of bar chord shapes in all positions. A section for the advanced player listing the moveable shapes for chords widely used by Jazz guitarists. Other sections contain important music theory for the guitarist including scales, keys and chord construction.